£2

BLOOD
OF THE
INNOCENT

TEÓFILO CABESTRERO

BLOOD
OF THE
INNOCENT

Victims of the Contras' War in Nicaragua

Translated from the Spanish
by Robert R. Barr

ORBIS BOOKS
Maryknoll, New York

CATHOLIC INSTITUTE FOR
INTERNATIONAL RELATIONS
London, England

The Catholic Foreign Mission Society of America (Maryknoll) recruits and trains people for overseas missionary service. Through Orbis Books Maryknoll aims to foster the international dialogue that is essential to mission. The books published, however, reflect the opinions of their authors and are not meant to represent the official position of the society.

Spanish original © 1985 by Teófilo Cabestrero
English translation © 1985 by Orbis Books, Maryknoll, NY 10545
All rights reserved
Manufactured in the United States of America

Manuscript editor: William H. Schlau

Library of Congress Cataloging in Publication Data
Cabestrero, Teófilo.
  Blood of the innocent.

  Translation of: Nicaragua.
  1. Nicaragua—Politics and government—1979-
2. Counterrevolutions—Nicaragua—History—20th
century.   3. Terrorism—Nicaragua—History—20th
century.   4. Military assistance, American—Nicaragua.
5. Interviews—Nicaragua.   I. Title.
F1528.C313   1985   972.85'053   85-13658
ISBN 0-88344-211-6 (pbk.)

Published in Great Britain by CIIR (Catholic Institute for International
Relations), 22 Coleman Fields, London N17AF

CIIR ISBN 0 946848 11 4

This chronicle of the shedding of innocent blood is dedicated to all the innocent persons who have been murdered, cut to pieces, raped, orphaned, abducted to Honduras by deception or threat, or attacked on their agricultural cooperatives. This chronicle belongs to those who have told me their story, and to those who have not, whether out of fear or because they are so many and their anguish is so inaccessible.

This chronicle of innocent blood is dedicated to the entire people of Nicaragua, to all of the peoples of Central America, and to their churches.

This chronicle of innocent blood is dedicated to those people in Mexico, Colombia, Panama, and Venezuela who have created the Contadora Group and who strive to realize peace by way of dialogue.

This chronicle of innocent blood is dedicated to those responsible for U.S. policy toward Nicaragua and Central America.

This chronicle of innocent blood is dedicated to the people of the United States of America, upon whom sorely depend the lives of thousands of poor men and women in Nicaragua—a land of the shedding of innocent blood.

Contents

HONDURAS

Rio Coco

• Ocotal   • Siuna

•Somotillo   • **Esteli**
              • Achuapa   • Bocana de Paiwas

              Lake
              Managua
                        Masaya   Bluefields•
Managua•
    Granada•

                          Lake
                          Nicaragua

PACIFIC
OCEAN
                              °.∘ Solentiname
                                    • SanCarlos

                                    CARIBBEAN SEA

                              COSTA RICA

Central
America

├──────┤ = 50 miles

NICARAGUA

Introduction

"This war, financed by the United States—we're the ones it's hurting, the helpless poor, the *campesinos*," said a *campesino* in the mountains of Nicaragua where the soldiers of the National Democratic Force (FDN)—the contras—make their incursions.

From February 4 to 20, 1985, I listened to the testimony of some sixty persons, civilians in the north of Nicaragua, who had themselves been the victims of kidnappings, bloody ambushes, rapes, and other kinds of assault by the contras, or who had survived the slaughter of their family or civilian friends.

I made a trip to the mountains and valleys along the Honduran border, to the Nicaraguan departments of Nueva Segovia and Chinandega. I visited towns and territories around Ocotal, Estelí, and Somotillo. In the north of the department of León, I visited a *campesino* cooperative that had just suffered a fiery, bloody attack.

The following chronicle is the story of my visit. It ends with the testimony of a priest and a nun from the United States who had seen the barbarities committed against the civilian population in other parts of Nicaragua—Paiwas, in the department of Matagalpa, and Siuna, in the department of Zelaya Norte.

Nicaragua is awash in the blood of the innocent. It is inundated by violations committed on the human rights, property, and lives of civilians. It is a land of war zones. This is the chronicle of some of that innocent blood—one small part of the exceedingly high price of the war in Nicaragua.

In no instance did I interview any member of the military or any politician. All of these testimonials come from civilians. And I moved from parish to parish. The priests and religious of the various locales were my only connections.

All of the accounts of the men and women I listened to, most of them poor, went straight into my note pad or my tape recorder and from there to these pages. I treated the words of these people with the sacred respect due the blood, death, grief, terror, desperation, and tears of the poor. The speakers are innocent, defenseless victims of a truly "dirty war." This chronicle is an attempt to gather up their innocent blood, their murdered or violated or shattered lives, their unknown tragedy. Innocence and blood have names—first names and last names, place names and the names of events. But they can be summed up in a scream—a scream demanding that this war stop, that peace come to the land.

During the days I was in Nicaragua recording accounts of kidnappings, threats, tortures, rapes, pillaging, murders, throat-slitting, demolition, arson, and massacres, told me by the civilian victims of the contras, I would listen to the evening "Voice of America" broadcasts, with their insistent apologias for the contras by President Reagan, who calls them "fighters for freedom and democracy."

For example, on February 6, 1985, after listening to two *campesina* women in Ocotal, each raped twice by contras before the eyes of their mother and their children, and after listening to four men who had been abducted by the contras, taken to Honduras, mistreated, and subjected to forced labor, I made myself listen to Mr. Reagan deliver his annual State of the Union Address, in which he sought to justify "support for the freedom fighters" of Nicaragua.

On February 16, I interviewed the parents of two young men who had been seized by the contras. One of them had his hands cut off and the other his skull crushed with a club ("the way you kill a snake," his father said). And I had just been in Estelí, where I heard from two survivors of an ambush of a truckload of civilians—some of the wounded had been finished off with bayonets, the others burned alive. Then that night of February 16 I listened to the rebroadcast of President Reagan's Saturday radio talk: "There are over fifteen thousand freedom fighters struggling for liberty and democracy in Nicaragua. . . . They are our brothers. How can we ignore them? How can we refuse them assistance when we know that ultimately their fight is our fight? How can we reject aid for them when this would be to betray our centuries-old dedication to supporting those who struggle for freedom? No, this is not only legal, it's actually consistent with our history." And he compared the contras of Nicaragua with the great Simón Bolívar the liberator, and Lafayette!

On March 1, a nun and a priest from the United States, who work in the region most threatened by contra incursions, told me how the contras murdered a number of Delegates of the Word there; then how they shot at point-blank range an eleven-year-old girl who screamed in terror, "Please don't kill me! Please don't!"; finally, how the contras raped a fourteen-year-old girl, slit her throat, cut off her head, then hung her head on a pole along the road as a lesson to passers-by. The priest told me, "I could see the contras didn't have a trace of humanity left. . . . It's like death swooping down, it's like Attila's hordes." The nun said, "To call the contras 'freedom fighters,' as President Reagan does, is a cruel joke. To me, it's cruel and immoral for the United States to give the contras support and aid." At the very moment they were telling me this, on March 1, 1985, Mr. Reagan happened to be addressing the Conservative Political Action Conference: "These freedom fighters are our brothers, and we owe them our help. You know the truth about them, you know who they're fighting and why. They are the moral equal of our Founding Fathers and the brave men and women of the French Resistance. We cannot turn away from them. For the struggle here is not right versus left, but right versus wrong."

There was a brutal contrast between what Mr. Reagan was saying and what the civilian victims of the contras and the North American priest and nun were telling me, and that severely depressed me. I wished that President Reagan could hear those men, those women, those children, those innocent victims of his "freedom fighters." And I wished that he would listen to the priest and the nun, U.S. citizens who are surely trustworthy when it comes to testifying about the war in Nicaragua.

Public opinion in the United States has already been offended by certain violations of human rights on the part of the contras. *America's Watch,* published in Washington, in a report on "violations of the laws of war by both parties in Nicaragua" (March 5, 1985), assures readers that the National Democratic Force is the contra group with the closest ties to the CIA and the one responsible for the most violations. It lists attacks on civilians, kidnappings, rapes, and terrorist raids on workers trying to bring in the coffee harvest. It accuses the United States of helping the contras to commit these abuses.

Similar reports concerning contra attacks on civilians have been published by other private human rights groups and have begun to circulate. The civilian victims of the areas that I visited speak of these abuses as standard procedure by the contras; in those areas the *campesinos* simply use the terms "contras" or "the Guards," (i.e., Somoza's National Guard) to designate the FDN forces.

I was struck by the great detail with which the *campesinos,* who always spoke to me with grief and sometimes with terror and tears, remembered all these events, all the things that they themselves, their families, their cooperatives, or their communities had suffered. They recalled everything with minute exactness, even when they were telling me things that had happened two or three years before. And they knew the importance of an exact account. They knew that this was history. A survivor of a massacre near Wiwilí, a man whose whole being spoke of grief, told me, "You see, I'm alive to tell the tale so that the world will know."

And so I have decided to leave the accounts of my "witnesses"— the suffering, the martyred—untouched, right down to the least details. I shall accord these accounts the respect due legal documents or the Acts of the Martyrs. For this is what they are. They are the truthful records of the spilling of innocent blood. They constitute testimony that the grief and human pain of Nicaragua are more noble and worthy of respect, more daily, more concrete, and more complex—and the injustice of this war more cruel and inhuman—than the world dreams.

With all of those who believe in the gospel of Jesus Christ, and with all of those who believe that Jesus of Nazareth is the Son of God and that the risen Lord was once crucified and that it is he who holds the final power to raise all of the crucified to life, I can already hear his words to us on the day of judgment: "I was innocent in Nicaragua. I was poor and defenseless. And I was kidnapped to Honduras. I was afraid of death threats. I was afraid when they burned my house. I was a reading teacher. I was a minister of the Word of God. I was seeking to render some service in the community. And they killed me with slashes of the knife. They raped me. They left me an orphan when I was six days old, and their amusement was to shoot me point-blank and laugh at me, a child screaming in terror. They cut my throat. They burned me alive. They slaughtered me."

And with those who believe that there is a great deal more in this innocent blood than meets the eye, I know that the Lord will ask us: "What did you do about it?"

The innocent blood of Christ's sisters and brothers cries out from the earth of Nicaragua.

1

Somotillo:
Campesino Leaders Murdered,
Compesinos Massacred

Somotillo—where the interviews transcribed in this section were held—is a region in the northern part of the department of Chinandega. The town of Somotillo is situated seven kilometers from the Honduran border. At 9:30 P.M. on the evening I arrived in the town, I heard a loud explosion, like a grenade or mortar fire, followed by shots. Then there was silence the remainder of the night. Later I found out that the contras had blown up a civilian vehicle with a Claymore mine (made in the United States). The mine had exploded, but the vehicle had kept going, and the contras had fired at it. There were no victims. This happened two kilometers from Somotillo. The man driving the vehicle was the civil officer in charge of a road-building project financed by Switzerland; he was returning to the little town of Somotillo. The road will be a great boon to the progress of the region all around.

I spent peaceful nights in Somotillo after that. In the daytime I would take the testimony of the civilian victims in the regions around Jiñocuao and Los Limones, and in the towns in the region of Santo Tomás, San Pedro, and San Francisco del Norte, in the mountains along the Honduran border where the Guasaule flows. I learned that the explosion that first night had not been part of any military operation. It was an act of terrorism against the civilian

5

population, one of a series that I was soon to learn of in that northern area of the department of Chinandega. I had been told that the area was where the contras had begun their bloody actions against civilians in 1980 and 1981. Now there was out-and-out war, and the actions were intensifying.

I left the cotton fields of Chinandega, at the foot of the gigantic San Cristóbal volcano. The harvest was winding down. I crossed the plantations, went through some heavily guarded checkpoints, and came to an extremely dry, dusty region—Somotillo country in winter. Here, under a scorching sun, I saw poverty bare—the lean and cadaverous poverty of a rocky region where people live in huts of sticks and clay. I saw crowds of children. There was some livestock (pigs, chickens, rabbits). I was told that there was corn and sorghum, or *miyon* ("animal feed and people food"), and, higher up, kidney beans. I saw cattle. And I saw cattle in Honduras, as I came several times within a stone's throw from the frontier. Everything was calm. "It was more dangerous around here when Alvarez Martínez was running the Honduran army," I was told. "We were more afraid of Honduran army mortar fire than contra attacks."

I saw leafy mangos and superb ceibas and *guanacastes*, survivors of the old forests. And I saw the cactus lay its yellow flower upon the earth like a touch of tenderness in the midst of the drought and the heartbreak. I contemplated the drama of the poor, who were giving up their land and homes to gather in barrios and settlements—"running from the bands of Guards, and scared to death," as they said.

Here too I met Dominican Father Vincente, from North America, from San Francisco. "The contras are destroying the people," Father Vicente told me. "Their projects, their efforts, their organization, their leaders—a whole people is being destroyed." He had come to work in the area for a few months and then he was going to return to the United States to appeal for solidarity with the people of Nicaragua. "The people of the United States have to be told," he said. "They have to open their eyes to the destruction financed and supported by President Reagan's policy. The people of the United States must accept their responsibility for this deceitful policy."

That U.S. priest witnessed the twenty-six interviews I held in his area. "I want to listen," he told me, "and then take the truth back to the United States."

GEORGINO ANDRADE

"We didn't expect this here. It was extremely surprising to us that they murdered Georgino. And so brutally! It was peaceful in the vicinity at the time; we felt no need to defend ourselves or arm. There was hardly a rifle for each village. And they sneaked up and killed our Georgino, our leader, our brother," said a man from El Nancital, a little village in the township of San Francisco del Norte. We were waiting for the arrival of Máximo Andrade, Georgino's brother, at a place where Delegates of the Word from all over the countryside were beginning to assemble to celebrate a prayer vigil for peace.

Georgino Andrade was murdered in El Nancital on May 18, 1980. The great National Literacy crusade was sweeping forward. In all areas of Nicaragua nearly one hundred thousand reading teachers were teaching an illiterate people to read and write. Georgino, who was a *campesino*, was enthusiastic about his job as Literacy Coordinator in the area. When he heard about the threats against the young reading teachers, he would say, "Over my dead body. Just let them try to touch one."

"Yes, they came for Georgino," recalled young José Ignacio Bustos, who had been with him when the contras broke into his house and dragged him off. "Georgino was a humble fellow, devoted to his people's progress through the government's programs. He had five children, from two months to seven years old. And he used to say they'd see the fruit of his labors. He was a great companion. He was in on everything. The killers knew Georgino was that way. That's why they came after him and killed him. He was twenty-nine."

Besides his job as Literacy Coordinator, Georgino had been responsible for the people's militia, which was just getting under way. He also worked for the church and the Christian community. He was getting ready to go to a community meeting when the contras came for him. He was on his way to celebrate the Word of God with the community. Instead, he was taken to celebrate his passion and death.

I first spoke with Máximo Andrade, Georgino's brother and a Delegate of the Word, when we met by agreement one evening on the dusty road he had to take to a community meeting. Laconic and serious, his face leathered by the wind and sun, a true *campesino* of the mountains, Máximo arrived at our rendez-vous on horseback and told me his story.

"It was a Sunday. Sunday evenings we'd celebrate the word of God in a school. Georgino was home with a specialist working on the Literacy Crusade. They were getting ready to sit down to supper. Then they were going to the celebration. Supper was on the table when four contras suddenly appeared in the house with others outside—sixteen all told. Georgino's wife saw them first, but she didn't know who they were, and she called to him: 'Somebody to see you!' He could tell who they were as soon as they started talking. So they grabbed him and tied him up. He asked them why they would want to tie him up; he wasn't a crook! They took him outside and went off with him. They took the literacy specialist too, and headed for my dad's house, next door to Georgino's. That was when I came along. Right away I realized what had happened, before I got to my dad's house, while I was still only as far as Georgino's. And when I got to my dad's house I could see the posters torn off the walls and lying in pieces all over the ground. They'd taken Georgino and the one from the Literacy Crusade. I ran to the school and told everybody there, all together for the celebration, that I thought we all ought to just go outside and face them. But we had no guns and they were armed. We couldn't do a thing. I went to Georgino's house and there was the supper on the table. I went looking up and down the roads. No sign of him. All night we looked for him. We still hoped they might let him go. When it was light we looked everywhere. It was May, and it got light early. Then we met some workers, who told us they'd found him, two kilometers away, in El Nancital. They'd killed him down there. There were sixteen slashes in his body—in his throat, in his chest, and in the back of his neck. They'd killed him with knives; that's why we hadn't heard any shots."

José Ignacio Bustos told how some contras had gone off with Georgino, while others made him, José, lead them to the health station. There they stole drugs and rations. "They burned the posters. They stole the CDS [Sandinista Defense Committee] money and headed straight for Honduras," seven kilometers away.

I asked Máximo Andrade what the effect of the murder was. "Everybody was scared to death," he answered. "We'd never had any problems like this. So they thought it must have been something personal at first. But then they saw it was against the process of the new government, the people's process. They saw that it was against the Literacy Crusade. Georgino was a person of great quality and talent. He was a generous man. They murdered him to strike a blow at the whole community, at the literacy campaign, at a process being run by and for the people. Just because he worked for the welfare of the community, just because he worked for change, so that poor people could finally get ahead, for social change that would benefit the community, so there'd be roads and schools. The people felt attacked, and they were afraid. But they reacted. We're reacting. The people got more involved in the defense committees, in the militias, in the Literacy Crusade. This is what the contras got out of it! This was the fruit of what the contras did."

Georgino's murder aroused great indignation in Nicaragua and a great awareness that the contra bands were enemies of the people. The people saw the contra assault on the literacy campaign as criminal sabotage. What the contras got out of this murder was the contempt of the people, who had almost all been affected and helped in some way by the National Literacy Crusade—members of nearly every family in Nicaragua either taught in the literacy campaign or received instruction from it. In Georgino's murder people could see who the contras were and what they were after. With Georgino's innocent blood, a story began. That story is still unfolding today.

ROSENDO GARCÍA

After hearing the story of Georgino Andrade, I learned how his had become the first in a string of murders of *campesino* leaders by the contras all over the extreme northwestern part of the country. The contras murdered only the leaders who had some connection with the church. Either the leaders were active in church work themselves, or their children or brothers or sisters were Delegates of the Word. The victims were always devout individuals from religious families, and the church had provided the impulse for the training of these rural leaders. It was not hard for me to find their families. All I had to do was ask a priest where they lived.

Berta Robelo de García is the widow of one of these murdered *campesino* leaders, Rosendo García. When I spoke with her, it was four years to the day since the murder, and her eyes still had a vacant look. They filled with tears when she told me how the contras had abused them and taken her husband away to kill him.

"When they tied him up they asked him what he'd done with the animals—a yoke of oxen he had. He told them he didn't have any. So they said that first they'd take his life, then they'd take the animals. They beat him; then they cut his ear off. There he was, all blood-soaked. They told us that if we'd give them everything we had they'd let him go. We gave them everything we had, and they took it all with them, but they took him too. They didn't leave me a single thing, not so much as a plate to eat from. They wiped us out. We had this little farm my mother'd left us, we'd had all our kids there, and now we didn't even have that. We came here to Somotillo. We were scared. Now I have no one to go to work; I have nothing at all."

Berta Robelo de García spoke slowly, as if it hurt her to talk. She was with her sister Corina and Corina's husband, Rosendo's brother. We were in the poorest of hovels, all sticks and straw, in a barrio that had been thrown up on the outskirts of Somotillo for refugees from the areas most affected by the contra attacks. A group of children had gathered at the doorway, but the adults did not hesitate in speaking of the atrocities while the children listened. The children of these parts of Nicaragua know all manner of "bloody stories" about the contras.

Berta went on. "We were living in the village of Las Aguas, near El Cuadro, on the banks of the Guasaule. We had a peaceful life. My husband worked four watermelon patches. Some of the fruit was already ripening. He had a good head on his shoulders, and he'd do anything you asked him to. He was a real community servant. He worked with the church. He joined the militia too. He was in charge of the militia when they were starting it up around where we lived—when they had to start watching out for the contra bands that'd come in to rob and steal—and started defending community property a little. But my husband didn't have a gun when the contras came. A *campesino* machete was all he had.

"It was February 13, 1981. We were home. Rosendo had been to a meeting and had gone out to tend to some seed that needed watering. He'd finished that, and we ate supper and went to bed. After we were in bed, they came, those contras. It must have been about nine or ten o'clock. There were a number of them, and they talked to him from outside. They told him to come out; they told him they had a job they wanted him to go on. I told him not to go out. Then they insisted so much, they called him their buddy, and they said they needed him for this 'mission.' So he got up, put his clothes on, put his sandals on, and went out. He had his machete in his hand. He went out, and they grabbed him; they took his machete away; they tied him up and beat him. They cut off his ear with a bayonet. After they cut off his ear they beat him some more, till he was all bloody. I saw it all. I was right there, and they beat him and pushed him back through the doorway. Four of them came in behind him. They wore clothes like his buddies, but they weren't his buddies. I didn't know any of them. They were armed.

"So they had him tied up, then they grabbed me. They beat me and told me they were going to slit my throat. They beat me with the rifles they had and put a knife to my throat, one of those knives they carry. They told me they were going to cut my throat, but right at that moment one of them—it must have been the one in charge of the others—came into the room where I slept with my children and said to the guy with the knife, 'Let the woman alone, let her finish raising her kids.' The children were really little then."

I asked her how many children she had and how old they had been when the contras had come. She thought a minute. Her sister helped her: "Leonardo was one; Leónidas, five; Margarita, ten; and Luís Abel, twelve. Luís Abel high-tailed it out of the house when he heard the talking and saw his daddy all tied up and bloody.

Berta went on: "He told them they could beat him up all they wanted, but they had no right to do it; he hadn't done anything wrong; he hadn't done anything to them that they should beat him like that; he made his living working. And when they told him they were going to kill him, he told them they might as well do it right there. I was right there; I heard everything. Then they told him they were going to take everything he had and let him live. And he told me, 'Give them everything in the house; you need me more than you need your stuff.' But they took everything and him too. When they took him away what I did was come here, where my sister lives."

Berta's sister Corina went on with the story. "I lived right nearby. I could hear everything from my house in the still of the night. And I saw it too. The moon was bright as daylight. When I heard them tell him, 'Get up, old buddy, we're going on assignment,' that was when he got up. When he got up, you can be sure he had his machete in his hand. Then he opened the door and they told him, 'Drop that machete.' I heard the machete drop. Then they took him outside, tied him up, and beat him. When they took him back into the house he was all beaten up. Then little Luís Abel ran out of the house, and they said, 'Look at that little goddamsonofabitch run.' And they came all the way up to my house, right by the side of the house before they went through a garden gate and left and kept going, since they saw the others were taking Rosendo away. But I saw that there were three of them still there, covering the others' retreat. When my sister came out she didn't see them. When she got to my house, crying, she told me, 'Sissy, they've got Rosendo!' 'Yes,' I said, 'I can see and hear the whole thing, but don't make a scene because there're three of them still there.' They already had Rosendo off somewhere by then, and the two of us stayed alone in the house, all night. There were lots of them. I saw about eighteen or twenty. I could see them perfectly. The moon was bright as day."

Berta added: "We spent the whole night afraid they might come back, or thinking they might be hiding somewhere looking to see what we were doing. If they came back, we could see they'd just kill us on the spot. Where in the world would we go? But sometimes we thought maybe they'd let him go and he'd come back. That's how we spent the whole night. And when we could see daylight we went looking for him. It didn't take long to find him, right along the river. He was still tied up, face down. His throat was cut. We wanted to go right up to him, but we were afraid—he was on the other side of the stream, in Honduran territory. So we came home and my sister went out to get some people to go over to the other side with us. So we went across. We went across to get him. He was face down, with his throat cut, and still with his hands tied behind his back. His clothes were all wet, and all over burrs—you know, those little burrs that stick to your clothes? God knows where they'd been with him. There aren't those burrs on our side of the river. They threw him on the river bank after they killed him so we'd find him. His body was all over bruises and cuts. As if they'd kept sticking him in the belly with a knife or bayonet."

Corina said she hadn't dared look at him. It would have been too horrible to see him thrown on his face out there with his throat cut. His widow finished the story: "I looked at him, though. I was his wife; I had to look at him. I just stayed there till his brother came to carry him back to this side, to Somotillo. I had to decide if I wanted him taken to Somotillo or if we'd have the wake at home. But I was scared, so scared—and people told me they might come back and kill my little boy. So I said that if I had to be alone at night I'd do better to take him to town. So we just came to town."

I asked Corina what she would do if peace came. "If peace comes," she said, "we'll go back. It'd be wonderful to plant, harvest, and feed the kids." For a single instant, the light of hope came into her eyes. I was gradually learning that every murder struck down not only a leader but crushed his family, which sometimes broke up, and the community, which, deprived of irreplaceable leaders, often collapsed. "This is Intelligence doing this," the relatives of one of the leaders told me. "These are crimes against the people."

PRESENTACIÓN PONCE

A month after Rosendo García's murder, the contras spilled the blood of another *campesino* leader in the same region. His name was Presentación Ponce. The whole countryside was struck with horror and indignation. Ponce was much appreciated for his services and his upstanding character. And then there was the way in which he was killed.

Before killing Ponce, the contras had abducted two Dominican priests working in the area. One of them, Father Angel Arnaiz, told me what had happened.

"That night, March 18, 1981, my confrère, Father Rolando Ugalde, from Costa Rica, and I were holding a vigil celebration for the feast of Saint Joseph. The whole village had turned out, and the celebration was a merry affair. After it was over we were busy driving people back to their houses in a van that'd been lent us. We'd made two trips. It was 11:00 P.M., and we were chatting at the door of a house along the road, near the river. Suddenly we heard, 'Hands up!' I thought it was a joke—some of the people from the celebration. But they shouted louder: 'Hands up!' I was so surprised—they were serious! 'Hit the deck!' we were told. We lay down on the ground, very quickly, face down, and the one that seemed like the leader searched us, to see if we had guns. We didn't. Two or three more came up and picked our pockets. They took quite a bit of money from Father Rolando, Costa Rican money and some dollars. He had been planning to use it to set up a church office. I didn't have any money, but they stole my pocket watch. I told them it was a family keepsake, but they took it anyway. By then they knew we were priests—they'd asked a girl who'd been speaking with us, and she'd told them we were priests and they'd better respect us. But they threw us on the ground, robbed us, and threatened to kill us. They made us keep our faces against the ground, and they went into the house to see what there was to steal. They took everything they could carry and then told everybody they were going to take us to the river and kill us.

"Then they made Father Rolando drive them off in the van. A *campesino* called Varela went along as a guide. Another *campesino* they had along, who was handcuffed, and I had to get into the back of the van, and the contras got in with us. We had to lie face down in the truck for the trip. They let me put my hands under my face, but the handcuffed campesino had his face smashed on the floor of the van every time we hit a bump. I couldn't imagine why they held a rifle barrel against my back and kept jabbing me with it. I could see our captors' boots all around. Must have been about eight men.

"We went about three kilometers, and they made Father Rolando stop and get in the back of the van. They handcuffed both of us, and some of them stayed in the van guarding us while the others disappeared. We stayed there a while, in the quiet and the dark, until we heard two shots nearby and our guards left on the run. We were frightened and puzzled. We didn't know what had happened. We wondered if they were coming back, or if somebody was still guarding us, or if they'd set a bomb or whatever. I wanted to find out, and I managed to get free and untie Rolando and the second *campesino*. We didn't know where the shots had come from, so we ran back to the house we'd been taken from. There was no one there. Everyone had gone up the hill. I shouted that we were Father

Ángel and Father Rolando and that we were back, but they didn't know whether it was really us; they thought it might be a trap and that if they came back down they would be caught and killed. So I moved closer to their hiding places. They saw me and came down. Then they told me they'd been told that we were going to be taken to the river and killed, and they'd been afraid. Then we learned that they'd murdered Presentación Ponce—a fine person, a servant of the community. He was a forty-six-year-old *campesino*, in charge of adult education in the area and responsible for the local militia. He was our great friend and helper in the pastoral work of the church, he and his whole family—two of them, a brother and a son of his, are Delegates of the Word."

Delegates of the Word of God are people who are selected for their natural qualities of leadership and who play a most important role in the development of religious and moral awareness in the community in their region. They are the pillars of the Catholic church in the countryside. They work in close cooperation with the priest, setting up and conducting worship services, including the celebration of the Word on Sundays and feast days, or religious festivals. That is, they reach the people—who are all very devout in the countryside—"where they live," reach them in their age-old traditions. Through their religious leadership and the training the church gives them, Delegates of the Word often become simply leaders of the community as such, organizing and developing services related to health, education, production, and consumption. In many areas of the Nicaraguan countryside all of the latter things have been greatly improved and developed with the coming of the revolution. Nicaragua, like other Latin American countries, has seen a great multiplication of these Delegates of the Word. They are the great strength of the Catholic church among the *campesino* people of Nicaragua, who constitute the majority of the population. In some areas Delegates of the Word have set up a network of promotional services, for "integral development," without abandoning their religious leadership and service to the community as ministerial pillars of the church. This is what has occurred in the regions of Somotillo and Chinandega, in the diocese of León.

The contras have killed a great number of Delegates of the Word. They literally persecute them. They hunt them and kill them. When the "Martyrology of the Delegates of the Word" is finally drawn up in Nicaragua, with precision and objectivity, it will become clear how much blood of the church has been shed at the hands of the contras. It will finally be seen how cruelly the contras have persecuted the church—something of which the world has as yet no notion.

Father Ángel himself took me to the Ponce home in Jiñocuao. We met Presentación's widow and three of their nine children. And I heard their stories on the very spot where the events had occurred.

Juan Pablo Ponce, twenty-six years old, Presentación's son: "My elder brother and I had been at a celebration of the Word that evening, over there in the religious community near the town square. It was about ten-thirty when the celebration was over, and we came home. My dad and mom and the kids were sleeping. We went to bed. Then about a half-hour later we heard the sound of a truck in the distance. It was the truck with the two Fathers. The contras were heading here. They came right to the house, and through that door right there we heard the voice of my dad's friend, a guy who used to live in Jiñocuao but didn't live here any more: 'Penta! This is Varela! I'm on a night mission. The guys say we're going on a mission tonight!' My dad recognized his friend's voice, but he just asked him why they wanted him at this time of night. Varela insisted, though, and kept calling him by his nickname, 'Penta.' And he said he was with the guys from the militia. My dad told us to open the door, but my brother and I said no, we shouldn't open the door, because we had the idea these weren't guys from the militia."

Juan Pablo's mom, María Luisa Ríos, Presentación Ponce's widow, interrupted: "I heard everything from here inside, where I was sleeping with my daughters, including the eighteen-months-old baby. I wanted to tell my husband not to open the door, but I was sick—I didn't feel well, and I just couldn't get up the strength to go and tell him."

Juan Pablo went on: "My dad insisted we open the door. I opened the door. A man barged in and smacked into me. He grabbed me and stuck what we call a *verdugilla,* a little dagger, up against my chest. He used me for a shield, and kept me between himself and dad. As the militia leader in the neighborhood, my dad had the only gun, and when he saw what was happening he grabbed it and pointed it at the guy. 'Take your hands off that boy,' my dad said, 'or you die.' The contra told him that if he fired the gun he'd hit me. Meanwhile another contra came in and grabbed my dad and wrestled with him for his gun. And another one came in—now there were three of them, with others outside. I didn't move because if I moved I figured I'd get stabbed. I just watched my dad wrestling with the two contras. And my brother, who had no weapon—what he did was run out of the house. All during this my mom and sisters were crying and crying. One of my sisters begged the contras to let dad go and not to hurt him and kept telling dad, 'Daddy, let them have it, give them the gun!' But he kept fighting with both of them. After a long fight they got the gun away from him. And they shot him with it. Two shots. My dad fell down and the bullets went through him into these two blocks in the wall there. Then they grabbed my mom. I don't know why."

It wasn't hard to see just what had happened and how. I saw where Presentación had fallen. A simple paper screen divided the single room of the house into two areas. On the clay wall against which Presentación's body had fallen there was a photo— Presentación, the serious, determined *campesino*. There was a little photo of his grave, and there were two little vases of plastic flowers.

Juan Pablo finished the story of the family tragedy this way: "When my father fell over dead, the two guys came up to about here, and the third one let me go. What I did was crouch down and cover my eyes and hope they'd murder me too. But they left. Everybody was crying, and they told them to keep still and shut the door. So they were gone, but I still thought they might come back and kill me too, so I ran for it, just in my trousers, barefoot. My other brother came back and just stood there, looking at my dad, murdered on the floor. Then my dad's two brothers came. They live practically next door. When my mother got up and found my dad stretched out on the floor and saw I was gone, she thought they'd kidnapped me, and so now it was worse for her than ever.

It hurt mom to tell the story. Weeping, she told me: "I knew they were coming to kill somebody and that nobody was going to be able to do anything about it. I couldn't do anything but just stay with my daughters and cry. After they killed dad one of them came in there where I was crying, with my daughters. And he looked for the guns my husband always kept there. He knew what he was looking for and where to look. 'I'll take these,' he said. And they left. Dad was dead. I came out here crying with the three girls, and when we saw that my son Juan Pablo wasn't here I thought they'd taken him. So I screamed, 'Leave me my little boy!' And one of them came back with a gun, pointed it at me, and said, 'Lie down and close those doors or we'll shoot you too!' And we just cried."

Then Ana Rosa interjected: "I was hiding under my bed because I thought they were going to do something to us too. After I heard the shots, I came out crying with my mom and we saw him lying in that corner."

Alfredo Ponce, fourteen, very small, but with a voice that had already changed, added: "I was sleeping there on that cot. The shots woke me up, and I jumped up and ran out behind the house. Then I came in again and saw my dad stretched out on the sack of wheat there, with his head against the wall. And I looked at my mom, who was in here after they were gone, the contras. They left as fast as they could go. They hit the road."

I also spoke with two of Presentación Ponce's brothers who live very near the house where all of this happened. Valentín Ponce, forty-seven, Delegate of the Word, told me that he saw the contras running away after the shots. "There were seven. I went over to my brother's house and saw him lying on the sack of wheat. I blessed him and took him off the sack. I propped him up on the floor."

Desiderio Ponce told me that their elder brother, Juan José Ponce, married, with nine children, had gone to work, after this, in the department of Río San Juan, in the south of Nicaragua, and that the contras had murdered him there in 1982. "They came by night. They took him and both of his boys. They killed all three."

Presentación Ponce's widow finally told me: "Here I am deserted. My husband is gone. My only consolation is that I still have these two big boys. And my only hope is that the ones who came to kill Dad—well, the Lord, not I, will judge them."

I was informed that among those who had committed the murder were Somozist National Guards, who knew the area well, as this was their native region. "Five hundred Guards left here for Honduras in 1979, at the triumph of the revolution. Some of their families live around here, and sometimes the Guards come at night to visit them." I noticed that there were no sentiments of revenge— nor had there been any reprisals by the Ponces or their pro-Sandinista neighbors against the families of the ex-Guards. The murder itself, however, continues to provoke the greatest indignation. Juan Pablo told me: "It's a rotten thing to do, put an innocent person to death who's working for the liberation of his people and his family. I think it was cowardly for them to murder him in front of all his children and his wife when we didn't have any way to defend him. This is what makes me mad about the way Dad died. They came and killed him just because he defended and served his community and to instill fear in the people of the countryside, so that they won't want to have guns and won't be able to defend themselves."

"What did the contras gain by this murder? What did the murder of this community leader in this region produce?" I asked. Valentín Ponce: "Since then we're better organized and better able to defend ourselves. Presentación was one of the first to join the defense committee. Nobody else wanted to. The day after he was shot there were twenty more."

Desiderio Ponce: "We've kept building and organizing. People have told me I should quit. Never. I don't care about the danger to myself. I kept at it for my fallen brother's kids and for my buddies. I volunteered as a replacement for my brother."

Ana Rosa Ponce: "When Daddy died we started working for the adult education program. That was one of the things he did."

Juan Pablo Ponce: "The contras didn't gain a thing. The community got mad, everybody got excited about the murder, and people organized and joined the militia here in the community. Dad's death just made for more commitment on the people's part, made for better community organization and stronger defense."

Father Ángel Arnaiz had the last word. "When I got to Presentación's house, I saw the whole drama—the family crying, the mom, the girls, the little guys. One of the big boys hadn't come home, and they were afraid he'd been killed. But what I remember best, and I'll never forget it, was seeing Presentación lying in that corner on a sack of wheat. The passage from John's Gospel hit me like a ton of bricks—that unless the grain of wheat falls and dies there'll be no harvest. To me, it looks like Presentación's death here had an effect something like the effect Rutilio Grande's death had on Archbishop Romero. Since that day I've made a vow not to leave here."

I think Father Ángel was renewing that vow before me because his eyes were full of tenderness and spirit.

ABEL QUINTERO

To get to the Quinteros' house I had to go through the intersection where the contras had killed Abel.

"He was killed March 23, 1981, five days after Presentación. The contras who killed Presentación killed my brother too," Vidal Quintero told me. Vidal was thirty. "We knew they were the same ones because my other brother, Sebastian, had a wrestling match with one after he'd dropped his gun and tried to run. And when we went to turn the gun in at the militia office in Somotillo we saw it had been registered to Presentación Ponce. It was the one the contras stole the night they murdered him!"

I saw four generations of Quinteros in the house by the time Vidal had told me his story. There were the parents, Don Luís Quintero and Doña Cipriana Ríos de Quintero, eighty-five and seventy-six respectively, who had had twelve children and now had fifty grandchildren and twelve great-grandchildren. Several of their children were making tiles and were setting them on the floor to dry. A number of their grandchildren and a few great-grandchildren were playing or were herding the animals away so that the conversation would not be disturbed.

While we were waiting for Vidal to be able to break away from his tile-making, the old father, an indefatigable conversationalist, informed me that Abel was forty when he was killed, that he was married and had six children, that he was the president of the Bernardino Díaz Farming Cooperative, and that he had been organizing the militia in the area around Los Limones. "That evening he was recruiting people for the cotton harvest. They were going to go out at three in the morning. He was willing to do anything. He was very capable. And he was devoted to the community good.

"There were rumors that the contras were looking for the leaders of the cooperatives," Don Luís said. And Julian, another of his children, twenty-eight, added: "They'd been waiting for him all day, where the road comes out onto the highway." Then Don Luís: "We heard the shots. And then I heard his brothers shouting. They'd been right with him. 'Dad! Come quick! They've killed Abel!' I went right over."

Doña Cipriana, a short woman with very light skin, all dressed in green, said: "I had a fainting spell. I fell over as if I were dead."

Don Luís: "When I got to him, there he was, lying on his face. I was carrying a lamp. Then a patrol car came up—my other boy had gone to report. 'Who's the dead person—do you know?' 'Yes—my son.' "

Vidal's story was short. "We left the house here together, Abel, Sebastián, and I. When we reached the highway the two of us here stopped and talked for a bit while my brother Abel stopped in at his house in Los Limones. We talked for several minutes there. And all of a sudden in front of us was a band of seven counterrevolutionaries. They were in olive drab and had garand rifles. It was really sudden because they shouted 'Hands up!' and another shouted 'Fire!' all at the same time, and they fired. We looked around for some place to dive, but Abel had a bullet in his head and dropped dead. One of them and my brother Sebastián had let go of their rifles and were wrestling. The others ran. I chased them up a little ways, but then I heard Sebastián shouting, and I came back to where they were wrestling. When I got there the contra was telling him to let him go, that they were the same and had no business killing each other! So my brother said if they were the same then why did they shoot at us. So the contra said that after all a person could make a mistake, couldn't he, we didn't have to take it so hard. My brother screamed that his brother was dead. I came up, and my brother looked at me and said something to me, and the contra got away from him and ran for it. He left his rifle. We ran after him a couple of kilometers, but we couldn't catch him. We went back and got the rifle that turned out to be the one they stole from Presentación, the same one that they'd killed him with a few days before that."

Don Luís added that the families of four Guards lived near the spot where his son had been killed. The Guards were now based in Honduras, but the families were still there. "The Nicaraguan officials took the families in for questioning, but let them go. Just because it was the Guards who did it was no reason to punish the parents." And he added, "No father is going to send his sons on a vendetta like that." Once more I could see that sacred respect, that absence of a desire for revenge.

"We saw that there was an operation going on to murder our leaders," Vidal said.

Don Luís acted as family spokesperson to tell me about the effect

Abel's murder had had on the family and the neighborhood. What had people's feelings been? "Here we got more courage and spirit to keep organizing. Now we're determined to the death. Well, we were to begin with. But now that this has happened we're even more so. And every last one of us is in on it, in on the political process. All my children, including the girls, and my wife and I. We're working in the cooperatves, and we're working to defend them. One's as stubborn as the next. And we're ready for anything. We can see they get all kinds of help from the U.S. government, which is powerful. To stand up to the U.S. government will take a little time. But if we have to we have to. Mr. Reagan's government ought to be ashamed—bullying a little country like this! And making up a bunch of lies about our process so they can keep bullying us! It's a downright shame! They ought to be ashamed. All we want is peace. All we want is to work and see the fruits of our efforts. And see our people develop. And all the more so with this government we've got now that's 100 percent for the poor. This government of ours is really with the poor. But that U.S. government! The danger for us isn't the Guard in Honduras. It's the U.S. government."

So spoke Don Luís Quintero, eighty-five years of age.

MASSACRE IN SAN FRANCISCO DEL NORTE

The year 1982 was one of great suffering in the towns and districts of the region of Somotillo along the Honduran border. The civilian population often came under mortar attack and other assaults. "Not only the contras attacked us," I was told. "The Honduran army would cover their retreat with a mortar barrage." The fierce, bloody facts spoke, too, in San Pedro, and in various bombardments of Santo Tomás del Nance (or del Norte), where the civilian population had come under repeated mortar bombardment.

In March 1984 a number of mortars fell on civilian housing in Santo Tomás. I went to visit the home of Doña Isaura. I saw the place where she had taken shelter along with a number of other persons, including a good many children. But a mortar fell so close to them that its fragments tore holes in the clothing that was hanging on the wall. A sister of Doña Isaura showed me the scar from the fragment wound in her arm and recounted to me how her little niece, Doña Isaura's eleven-month-old baby, was struck in the face by a fragment that passed between her cheekbone and her eye and entered her brain, killing her instantly as she lay in her mother's arms.

But the cruelest affair was that of San Francisco del Norte, the most remote of the townships of Somotillo, ten kilometers from the Honduran border, on July 24, 1982. The international press and part of the diplomatic corps in Managua—the ambassadors of Venezuela, Mexico, France, and Honduras, who visited the village the next day—called it the San Francisco Massacre, so vicious had been the fire power directed against a population without any military defense whatever, so appalling the cruelty with which the attackers had murdered (and "finished off" if they had only been wounded) fourteen young *campesinos* and students, and so horrible the terror and bloodshed with which they had succeeded in petrifying the population. The contras had cried, "Hurrah for the National Guard! Long live Somoza! Hurrah for the National Democratic Force!" and had painted these slogans on walls in graffiti that proclaimed themselves "Christians for Democracy" and declared that they had come to "combat communism with God and patriotism." The people there are still asking, "Do you massacre people in the name of God?"

I arrived in San Francisco del Norte from the town of Somotillo along the rocky road that snakes through the mountains along the Honduran frontier. Today the town is like a museum. Articles are displayed as evidence of the attack. One can see photographs of the young people who were massacred and visit the knoll where the young *campesinos* and students were riddled with bullets and bayoneted, where they had their throats slit, were mutilated, and were finished off with whole shells. One can see movies and stills of the terror and grief of the villagers, waking and burying fourteen corpses, some of which had their heads or arms or legs artificially attached, as these had been blown off or hacked off.

The people in San Francisco del Norte still talk about the "massacre," and the women still cry when they talk about how the contras killed their children. I interviewed ten eye-witnesses of what had happened.

Don Francisco Solano Barrera, sixty, shoemaker and carpenter, received me in his "workshop"—a corner behind his house all piled high with his things—while a good number of his fourteen children were having lunch in the house with their plates in their hands. In the shade of a mango tree, with its green fruit, Señor Barrera told his story: "After the July nineteenth festival, we were all by ourselves here. The army had gone off, every soldier. Only we civilians were left. Our only defense was a few members of the people's militia—*campesinos* and students. And 150 contras came, with mortars. It was like an earthquake."

Señor Barrera is a heavy man, and he had stripped to the waist because of the heat of the hour. "That was a massacre," he went on. "I saw plenty with my own eyes. A good number are still living, see? My son Reinaldo Barrera Carrasco fell in the massacre. He was twenty-seven. He was a good carpenter. He had a wife and brand-new baby. He and another boy I've got working here had gone off and volunteered. The boy here escaped the massacre because he ran off and hid in a shallow ditch. They tossed a grenade after him, but it went over his head and landed in front of him. Then a mortar blew him out of the ditch and dropped him like a dead body, but he was all in one piece. Reinaldo called to him, 'Come here, I'm only wounded!' My boy'd been shot, but he was still alive. He'd fallen on his face—then, the way you'd kill a snake with a club, the contras ran up to him and smashed his skull with a single blow. Little bones and brains went flying. God gave me courage. I watched his brains literally being knocked out. I came home for some linens. He had no face left. He was just a bloody skull. If my son had been fighting, I'd say okay. But this way—no."

And he told me about his wife, María del Socorro Carrasco, who was fifty-two and was in the care of physicians, having had a complete breakdown after the murder of her son Reinaldo in that fashion. Finally they showed me a photo. He had been a handsome boy.

Odilí Moncada de Espinoza received me in her home. I didn't ask her age—perhaps thirty-five. She is short, a bit hefty, with smooth skin. Her black hair was flowing loose on her pink blouse. Emotionally, she told me: "The Guard came in from Honduras. The army'd left here. There were only *campesinos* and students left, people from San Francisco. They knew my son was here—Luís Alberto Espinoza. He was fifteen and a freshman in high school. Well, the contras dropped in that morning.

"I heard, 'It's the Guard!' I looked out, and our people were running to the command post on the hill. But there was too big a band of them, and we had only about twenty-five or so. We held them off for only two and a half hours. We were mortared and mortared. We only had Czech rifles. It was no match. There were dead and there were wounded, and the contras came up and finished off the wounded. They smashed the skulls of some of the wounded. My boy they disembowelled. They disembowelled him and broke his arms; they cut out my boy's heart, and then they mutilated him."

She began to cry. She went on in spite of the tears that washed her fleshy, ruddy face: "Some of the others had their faces torn off. It was a really horrible thing. After all those murders they came here to my house and stole everything I had. They stole everything. They broke my mirrors, everything I had here. There was nothing left in one piece. They took clothes and everything, even my dead boy's clothes; then they went off with my husband. I was left alone with my little boy here. He was all I had. They went off with my husband for four months. You were always worried, you know— we lived in fear. 'Here they come, here they come!' every so often. See, we've got an army defending us now, and at that time we didn't. Besides, we weren't as wide-awake then as we are now. Now we're organized. For example I'm on a mothers' committee; we're working with a defense committee; we're doing what's called revolutionary vigilance. And this is how we live, organized, so those people won't get in here again. This is what we hope, and this is the result of that awful thing that happened. We can't let those people come and commit more atrocities. That was too much. They took my husband off barefoot and shirtless. Let him tell you what they did to him."

Doña Odilí introduced me to her husband, Constantino Espinoza, forty-five, dark, with glasses, and he began to speak: "I've had trouble since I was wounded; I have to wear glasses. . . . I lost five members of my family in that battle, the one that ended in the massacre—a son, a brother, two distant cousins, and one first cousin. Anybody they found still alive they smashed their skulls or cut their throats. They cut off my boy's hands; they opened him up; they made mincemeat out of him. . . . They dragged me off with six others. They dragged me off barefoot. We walked from nine in the morning till seven at night, about eighteen kilometers. We had our arms tied behind our backs. There were about two hundred contras. We got to a camp in Honduras, a place called Cacamuyá, Cacamuyá Mines, and they kept me prisoner there three months and two weeks. They had about three hundred men in that camp. I could see they were well equipped. They had plenty of hardware. The weaponry I saw there was United States "aid"—hand granades, mortars, "fifties," FALs—all new equipment that said 'USA' on it. And waterproof knapsacks, boots, everything. The treatment we got there was the worst. At night they'd take us out in the cold. It's ice-cold up there. No shirt, with our arms tied behind our backs, till morning. We'd be freezing to death. We ate once a day. We got a bath about once a month. Worst treatment possible. Those people have no culture, no respect for anyone's rights. All they know how to do is murder and steal. Sometimes they knocked us around—clubbed us and kicked us. And they'd 'interrogate' us, and tell us we've got communism down here and they're fighting communism. This is the way they talk. Sometimes they say something about the Bible, or religion, and they've got a slogan—'With God and patriotism we shall defeat communism.' But there aren't any priests or ministers there, because they just murder.

"After three months and two weeks they took me out of that prison and drove me to a place called Danlí. They've got a camp there in Danlí. It's a training school the counterrevolution has there. And after three weeks they took us back, in the same Honduran army trucks, something like the IFAs we've got here. But they weren't training us; they were hiding us during some kind of visit from somebody from the United States. I could see how the Honduran army and the contras are in cahoots. And that's how Reagan sends his aid to the contras, through the Honduran army, because they're in cahoots, the Honduran army and the contras. The U.S. aid isn't just equipment and weaponry, either—it's personnel. Even the contras told us that the ones advising them and training them are from the United States.

"After all that, they gave me a gun, dressed me up like them, and took me to Nicaragua to go on raids with them. But the third night I got away from them. How was I going to go on raids with people that'd killed my family? And they've got different ideals from ours. We fight for the poor. They don't. What they like to do is steal from our people and murder them. They're Somoza's old National

Guard, you know. And they act like it. They haven't changed. It's the same old system and the same old Guard—same old enemies of the people. Those guys don't have any ideals. And they respect nobody."

José Santos, thirty-eight, is tall, strong, with curly hair sticking out from under both sides of his baseball cap. He was missing a few teeth, but I could understand him perfectly. "I was captured with Constantino Espinoza. When they captured us they beat us with the FALs the contras have, and we headed for Honduras. We passed through a place they call El Jicaral. We stopped there about half-an-hour. From there they took us to the border. We went into Honduras, and they took us to their post in Cacamuyá. Then I was taken to Santa Rita. I was a month in Santa Rita and another month in Danlí, in a place they call La Lodoza. Then they took me back to Cacamuyá again. In La Lodoza I saw four foreign advisers—two Israelis and two Argentinians.

"The contras didn't care for us a bit. They said they were going to kill us. They were always dragging us out for questioning. They'd ask us questions and beat us. Every day they beat us. All those months they told us that if we'd join them they'd let us out. So to get out we finally said okay, if they'd let us out we'd join the contras. They let us out, gave us guns, and put us in a scouting party. That was when we hit the road. Every last one of us. Constantino Espinoza escaped December 3. I escaped a month later, January 3, 1983. I waited until night. I made sure I knew where the guards were posted. I waited until one guard dozed off, and I ran for all I was worth. Before, we were always on the lookout for a way to escape from the camps, but we never could because the Honduran army was always working with the contras. We were always surrounded by Honduran regulars. In fact two Honduran army lieutenants and one DIN lieutenant asked the contras to hand us over to them; they were going to get rid of us; they said we were Sandinistas and they couldn't have us there, said it was dumb to think they could make contras out of us. They asked the contra leaders to hand us over to them so they could kill us."

On the floor beside José Santos sat Arturo Espinoza, twenty-two. He told me how he was wounded by a mortar fragment. The contras kept calling to the people to come out of their houses, saying they'd been "liberated." Nobody took the bait. Everybody stayed locked inside. When the contras saw they were all alone in the street, they regrouped and left the village for Honduras. They took their captives with them. Arturo told me that when they dragged him off his mom came out into the street, crying and running up to the contras and shouting at them to take her too, or else kill her if they were going to take her boy. "I was dying," Arturo added. "I'd have died on the way for sure because air was getting into the wound and filling up my belly; I was all swelling up. When they saw that, they let me go."

On my way back from San Francisco del Norte, I had occasion to observe some of the more recent traces of the death and grief caused by the passage of the contras. We were invited into the house of a Señor Martínez; it was eight kilometers from Somotillo. His wife and her children told me that the Señor had died two days before my arrival in Somotillo, on February 8, 1985, a Saturday night. He had been literally frightened to death at the sight of ten contras surrounding him and threatening to kill him. "He had heart trouble," said his widow, a short, thin little woman. "He didn't work. Doctor's orders. He'd gone to bathe in a little brook, about ten in the morning."

"I went with my dad," José said. José was fourteen and had sparkling eyes. "I was walking along behind him. When I saw the contras I hid in the bushes. There were about ten of them. They had blue uniforms on. I saw them surround my dad. They held a bayonet to his throat and told them they were going to slit his throat. Then they told him they weren't going to kill him after all, but that they would if he said one single word about seeing them there."

The mother went on: "He came back scared stiff. He went to take a nap in the other house, but he knew the girl there had been threatened. The contras had said they were going to kill her. He turned back. He got as far as the house here."

"He just dropped dead," said one of the older boys. And he continued: "The night before [February 7, 1985], they raided around here. They made the farm owners lie down on the floor, they put handcuffs on them, and they took their livestock, eight thousand cordobas, and a gold necklace. They're bandits, that's all."

2

Ocotal:
Kidnapping,
Torture, Rape

In the city of Ocotal, in the department of Nueva Segovia, First Region, and in various of the surrounding districts and townships along the Honduran border, I interviewed no less than twenty-six persons who had suffered personal or collective kidnapping, rape, or torture, or who had had members of their family murdered— whole populations threatened and intimidated through actions against workers and private coffee-growers.

A chapter on kidnappings would be endless and endlessly varied. A "kidnapping" or "abduction" in Nicaragua today does not mean what it does in the rest of the world. Elsewhere a kidnapping is a terrorist act against some individual, generally important or wealthy, who is captured and held by force for economic or political ransom. In Nicaragua a kidnapping is an ongoing tactic of the contras, who operate in armed bands, go to homes, work places, and secondary roads, abduct civilians, and take them to their camps in Honduras. The victims are always civilians and poor. The contras ask no ransom. They seek to terrorize; they seek to punish those they consider to be "with the revolution." But they nearly always try to recruit people forcibly for their ranks, in order to send them back into Nicaragua, armed, to fight their own people. The population suffers from these kidnappings. They fear them. The kidnappings are a plague of terrorism inflicted by the contras on the defenseless poor. Most of those abducted have no other wish than to escape. Of those abducted from the areas near the Honduran border, more than 80 percent escape back into Nicaragua.

The kidnap victims' accounts reveal the character of the contras, their manner of speech, their behavior, their argumentation, their means and methods—and what the victims think about all of this.

TWO YOUNG ABDUCTEES

In the city of Ocotal I listened to a young man and a girl in separate interviews.

Benjamín Aguilar Bustamante, twenty-two, who works for Nicaraguan Oil, was abducted by the contras May 22, 1983. "I was on my way to Jalapa in a small truck. There were three of us. When we got to San Fernando we were intercepted by the contras. I jumped out of the truck, but one of the contras trained his AKA on me and I had to stop. Up ahead the contras had stopped a bus, local interurban transport, and were holding all the passengers. After we were out of the truck and in custody they burned our truck. Then they took us to a contra concentration camp. All the people from the bus were there too—about eighty people, old people, kids, women, everybody. They put us in a stockade, like cattle on a ranch.

"They used pictures of Pope John Paul II. They had posters and propaganda sheets with his picture on them. The contras made a big speech to us. They told us that Nicaragua was persecuting religion because we had a communist system. And they told us about U.S. support for the contras, and Honduran support. They told us they were doing us the honor of explaining all this to us. And they showed us the weaponry and equipment, all marked 'USA.' "

The boy spoke with meticulous attention to details. He even drew me a sketch of the region to help me follow what he was going to tell me next. "The contras picked people out for abduction. They were going to take the ones they picked to Honduras, and they gave the order that anyone trying to escape would be shot. They picked out twenty of us. I was one. Ten contras went along as guards. We were heading for a camp they've got in La Lodoza, in Honduras, where they were supposedly going to train us, then arm us, and we'd be joining their ranks. We walked all morning and into the afternoon. About four in the afternoon we came to a ravine, on the other side of the mountain. We took a rest. The contras killed a young steer and told us we were going to lug it to camp. But the Sandinista army was on the way, trailing the group. The contras spotted them and got all nervous and confused. Eight other guys and I saw our chance and ran for it. We went a little way around a crag up the mountain and hid all night. Next day we came back. I didn't see anything after we escaped and hid.

"I could see, all the time I went with them, how the majority of the contras that were with us were kidnapped *campesinos*. The contras have abducted a lot of *campesinos* and have lied to them and scared them. I was talking to the chief, and I told him, 'Let us go! Look, you're taking us by force. People you take by force'll only give you problems.' That bothered him. He pointed his gun at me as if he were going to kill me, but I studied him psychologically and I could see he couldn't really make up his mind to do that."

The girl who told me about her kidnapping by the contras didn't want to give me her name for fear of reprisals. "One day in June 1983, along about three in the afternoon, we were on our way back to Ocotal from Dipilto, three of us, in a jeep, plus the nurse and two boys. About two kilometers out of Dipilto they started machine gunning our jeep. It was the contras. I slipped down under the dashboard. They didn't stop us. We sped up. They were spread out for a kilometer along the road, so we had to do a kilometer under fire. I put myself in God's hands. I felt a jerk—they'd gotten the jeep with an RPG-7. And we slammed into a truck right at the entrance to a bridge they were dynamiting. The others jumped out, but I stayed in with another girl. They came up and told us to get out or they'd kill us. I got out. I was wounded. I could see about sixty contras in blue uniforms. They made us lie on the ground, face down. Then they pulled us up. 'March!' they said. But then suddenly they said, 'Hit the dirt!' And the bridge blew up. I was petrified. We started marching again. I was crying. I looked at one of the guys and he was all bloody. We kept going and kept going. I was still crying. I asked them where they were taking us. They said to where the chief was. About nine o'clock at night it started to rain. The rain came down in sheets, and about eleven o'clock they decided to stop for the night. We were going to spend the night with the contras. My girl friends and I were scared to death. But about four in the morning we all started out again. I cried and cried and begged them to let us go. They kept saying they had to follow the chief's orders. We walked till the end of the next day without anything to eat. We were exhausted. Finally we got to a camp.

"There were over three hundred contras in the camp. I could see they all had plenty of guns, along with some beautiful rain gear. Must have been from the United States. They were machine-embroidered 'FDN.' A lot of them carried rosaries. When we got to the camp they gave us some beans and guinea bananas. After a little they took us to a building where they had heaps of other people. They separated us—the nurse, the wounded boy, and me—from the others. We three never saw the others after that. And we got ready to spend another night with the contras. It was awful, you know? They could have done anything they wanted to us. All we could do was pray.

"At daybreak they came back to get us up and took us to camp headquarters. They took my purse. They 'registered' us and started 'interrogating' us. They tried to 'conscientize' us. They explained how they were all fighting to free us from 'communism in Nicaragua.' Great way to free us, I thought. Besides, they were freeing us from a phantasm they had in their heads, for ideological convenience. They were freeing us from what we didn't need to be freed from. What they told us was just a huge lie. But I was still scared and frightened. These thoughts kept coming into my head, but they didn't make things any easier. I just wanted to know what they were going to do to us and when this horrible nightmare was going to be over. Well, they questioned us over and over. They'd take one of us, then the other, then the other. We told them over and over again that we didn't want to stay. They spent the whole day like that, trying to persuade us. They never questioned us in a group. We were always separated. Sunday, at noon or so, one came and asked, 'Well, what have you decided?' We said, 'To go home.' They told us, 'Impossible. You'll be staying.' I started crying again. I was in a state of collapse. He came back half-an-hour later. They had to mobilize, and we were in the way. He told us they were going to let us go but that they were going to keep on fighting and were going to win. Then I saw how a lot of them were starting to move out, practically running away. We heard, 'Civilians up and out!' And we moved out. It was more torture—they kept telling us, 'C'mon, move!' and things like that. We were tense. At about five we got to a place where they told us to go on alone.

"We started out, the three of us. It began to rain again. We'd slip and fall. The guy was wounded and all. Toward midnight we had to stop. We just couldn't go on. And we didn't know where we were. We decided to spend the night in the mountains. Another nightmare. At about 3 A.M. we started out again. The other girl'd lost her shoes. We were crying. I don't even want to remember. Our families were looking for us. They thought we were dead. It's been five months, but it's like it was yesterday. It crushed me. Every night for five months I've dreamt they're after me, that they're tossing a bomb at me. I'm so scared! I still don't go out. No more trips for me."

TOTOGALPA: VILLAGE PARALYZED BY FEAR

I spent a whole day in Totogalpa and spoke with a number of families. I heard the stories of several kidnap victims who had escaped and spoke with the parish priest, a member of the Foreign Missions Society of Canada, Father Henri J. Coursol.

Totogalpa, a township in the vicinity of Ocotal, is at the foot of the international highway to Honduras, at the Las Manos border crossing. The little village numbers some ninety houses, all very poor. Most are of clay. Here and there in the vicinity are some thirty hamlets and groups of houses. The total population is about nine thousand, all Amerindians. More than two hundred persons from this small area have been abducted by the contras.

The land around Totogalpa is rocky and infertile. "It's a little village that doesn't produce anything," said the village sage, an eighty-year-old woman, a sparkling conversationalist. Most of the population live on what they manage to earn as agricultural day laborers, picking coffee or doing other farm or ranch work. But the abductions during the coffee harvest have finally terrorized the people to the point where many are no longer willing to do the work, and so are deprived of the main source of their annual income.

There is no military detachment assigned to the village, only a few civilians in the militia. Yet the village has been attacked by contra mortar barrage and machine-gun fire four times. This is a periodic practice on the part of the contras to cow the people and terrorize an area they need to make their runs down from the ridges where they hold up. This is the quickest way back to Honduras after a strike. The people are terrified. They trust no one. They lock their doors at sunset—6 P.M. or so. "You never know," they whisper. "If they see an open door they can get in. They do everything at night."

"Last Christmas," the parish priest told me, "we celebrated 'Midnight Mass' at nine in the evening. Thirty people came. The village is paralyzed by fear. Some sleep in a different house every night." And he told me of the anguish suffered here whenever the contras came with their machine guns or launched their mortar barrages, which could go on for as long as twenty minutes. He told me also about his ongoing work with the civilian population, trying to help them cope with ambushes, woundings, and deaths.

Terror has spread all through the region. Five schools have closed, after warnings by the contras that teachers showing up for work would be killed. Several adult education teachers have been abducted. Several Delegates of the Word and a number of catechists, of whom there are 180 in the parish, have also suffered abduction. The parish coordinator of the Delegates of the Word, Manuel López Blandón, thirty-four, recounted to me—in the shade of a magnificent, tall ceiba tree—how in October 1983, at six in the morning, armed contras came to his house and demanded foodstuffs. They roused him and demanded he supply them with provisions and guide them to a certain mountain. "That was a bunch of barbarians, for sure—all in blue, and with 'FDN' stenciled on their shirts. They weren't out kidnapping that day; they were just on their way to their own homes for a visit—all armed. They asked me why I couldn't see that the Nicaraguan government was slipping into Marxism-Leninism and persecuting religion. I answered them that from my experience as coordinator it seemed to me that the church around here was functioning as well or better than before— we always had a celebration of the Word. And when they asked me if there were people in this community who believed in God, I told them yes, that in my community we all believed in God, and lived for God and that that was why we were doing what we were doing, because God protected us every instant. They said that the Nicaraguan government was killing the faith in Nicaragua. I could see they were mixed up. They'd been fed a good big dose of propaganda. I was afraid that day. But what I was afraid of were the weapons. And I told myself, yes, I was afraid of the weapons, because you never knew what somebody with a weapon in their hand would do—but I didn't fear the person *with* the weapon because we're all equals. Yes, my wife and children felt afraid when the contras went off with me. They took sixteen of the people from the community that same year. It was really sad. Some came back in a week and some came back in two. But one died and another was wounded."

"They Have to Drag Us Off by Brute Force"

I heard long stories of abductions in Totogalpa, like that of Coronado Muñoz Zamora, an Amerindian. "I'm married with five kids." He spoke softly, slowly, as if he didn't have a great deal of strength; he had recently been operated on for the damage done when a horse had kicked him in the stomach. "The devil got into that horse!" he would say. "They told me to kill him, but I'm not going to kill him; he's an innocent animal."

As we sat together in his poor hut, with three rickety old beds and a sack of corn, Coronado recounted to me, in great detail, all the things he had gone through. "The Literacy Crusade was on," he said. "I was a coordinator. I helped the reading teachers a lot, and the contras didn't like that. Pretty soon they came looking for me. They were going to kill me. I lived in Callantú Valley—worked there as a night watchman in a high school. Plenty of times I had to head for the hills. I slept in the mountains, slept in the rain, got bitten by mosquitos. It was hell. They came looking for me. They were going to take me. But then some friends put in a good word for me—they told them I was a good guy and didn't bother anybody. So they let me alone for a while. But a little later they came and got me.

"They came for me November 25, 1984. They got here at 8:30 P.M. They stopped at every house. Six of them would go up to a house, armed to the teeth, and say, 'So-and-So, old buddy, c'mon, we gotta have a chat.' I could tell they were contras. I'm not dumb you know. I know our army talk and I know theirs. 'I'm sick,' I said. 'Aw, c'mon, get up—you don't wanta see your house burn down, now, do you?' And they dragged me outside. I begged them not to take me; I told them I was alone and my kids were sick. They wanted to take my little brother, too, and one of my daughters. But my daughter was sleeping with her little sister and I told them I had that little girl there and she was sick, and they left her there. 'Well, take me, then,' I said, because my brother started crying.

"They already had thirty-eight people, from Río Abajo, from Yalaguina, and from Jocote. They had five from Terrero Grande. They were taking all of them. They said they'd already taken eighty, two weeks earlier. I marched with them for three days without anything to eat. They didn't give us a thing. We traveled by night. I was sick, with a headache, maybe from hunger. They had money with them, and they'd send us in places to buy bread, bags of bread, chickens. They ate fine, and they let us go hungry: a little piece of tortilla, and then nothing for supper.

"They told us they were taking us to Honduras, to train us to attack our people. They told us they were going to win, that the Nicaraguan army was crazy, and that they'd win in a month. They told us they'd already just about won, and all they had to do was fight a little bit more and everything'd be okay. They told us they were going to give us money so we could have a good life, and we'd be back from Honduras with plenty of money for our families. They told us we couldn't have anything here in Nicaragua because everything was rationed. They said they had all sorts of stuff in Honduras. 'The lame walk and the blind see up there. 'We've got hot-shot doctors!' they told us. They told us that the U.S. was their main support, that the U.S. was going to give them a lot of aid, and that they were going to win. They told us that all their equipment was from the U.S.—good stuff, good knapsacks, good raincoats, and all the rest of it. They threatened us, too—told us if we tried to get away they'd cut our throats. They told us there was a kid who'd gotten away; he was a little rat; he'd run off down into a gorge and they were looking for him; if they found him, they were going to cut his throat; they weren't going to use a bullet because they didn't want to give away their whereabouts. They guarded us extra close because that young guy'd gotten away from them. One of them would be between every two of us, and when we went to sleep it was the same, so nobody'd escape. They had a big radio, and they used it to keep track of our army, so they could pay attention to which way to take. When they knew the army was around, they'd move only at night. Once they got us up at three in the morning and we had to hit the road. We were cold and hungry. At night we were lashed to one another with a tether so nobody'd high-tail it. But one day we came out on a path and the Nicaraguan army had an ambush waiting for us. The bullets started flying and everybody hit the dirt. I dived into a ravine. Unfortunately I knocked into one of the contras who'd had the same idea! 'Get the hell back up there!' he shouted at me. I had a heavy duffel bag. I climbed back up, got back out onto the road, and when I saw everybody flying every which way from our guys' ambush, I saw my chance. I ran for it. I shot down the gorge, fell, the duffel bag flew open, I left everything scattered, and I got away.

"I had a miserable time getting back. I got lost over and over. I was barefoot. And I ran into a number of the guys that'd been kidnapped. They'd all scattered when we'd run into the ambush. One of them fainted on us along the way. But we got some help at a few of the houses. They gave us coffee and tortillas. So I got home. My family was out of their minds. The kids had been crying. The little girl practically passed out with delight when she saw me. They thought I'd been killed.

"Since then we had another martyrdom, though, and after I got back, a lot of times we've had to head for the hills at night and leave the house empty and the animals untended. I'd stick the family in one house one day and another house the next day, and my brother and I would sleep up in the hills. We slept there a week once. Almost nothing to eat. Figured the contras were after us. Until we decided to move here. I feel a little better here. Now I've got this pain from the operation, though, from the horse kicking me, but that's not the same thing. That's something I'm willing to suffer—that's part of the reality of life."

Coronado added one more little recollection, and reflection. "The contras were drugged. And when they ran out of drugs they'd scrape a little gunpowder off some bunches of threads they'd pull out of some shells and eat that. They said it was to get high. They offered me some. 'Have some?' they said. 'No, thanks,' I said. 'Why not?' they said. 'I'm afraid it'll affect my brain,' I said. They talked a lot about being devout Catholics and how they believed in God and carried a Bible. They said the ones in Nicaragua right now didn't believe in God; they were communists. They said God was on their side because they believed in God. And they had medals on chains around their necks. Some of them prayed to Bishop Madrigal, and asked him to defend them in battle. Some of them would pray and make the sign of the cross before heading out on a mission. But I would say, 'What do you mean, you read the Bible, and then you screw people up like this?' Because we were all getting screwed; we were going with them against our will, we weren't volunteers, we'd been forced, we'd been abducted. I'd say, 'If you look at the Bible, how can you go around screwing people over this way?' I knew they were full of baloney. And I thought, 'How can these people be so fooled? They have to drag us away by brute force!' "

Forced Labor

Francisco López, twenty-seven, was abducted with forty of his companions on January 16, 1984, as they were harvesting coffee. They were and are civilians. Following is his testimony.

"Several of us from here, from Totogalpa, went to pick coffee. We were going to sleep in the ranch house up in the hills. But the very first night, when we went to bed, about 8 P.M., and turned out the light, all of a sudden about thirty contras came in, with their guns. They told us to get out of the house and line up, because we were all going to Honduras. As I say, there were forty of us, and they already had about eighteen from other ranches.

"We got to Honduras the next day, without anything to eat. We were around Las Dificultades. Finally they gave us a piece of biscuit and a little meat. That was all. The next morning, at about four, we headed for La Lodoza. We got there to the camp and a doctor told us that the contras were going to win in June. That was June of last year. They gave us a little piece of a tortilla—very little to eat—and made us go on forced marches loaded down with ammunition. Sometimes we'd be asleep and they'd get us up at night to carry water, provisions, food. They had their wounded there. They had a doctor treating them.

"We went through intensive training there. I was fat when I got there, but I was good and thin by the time we were through! We had basic training, and we had to 'present arms,' and all that business.

We had to obey all the instructor's orders. He might say, 'Kiss those stakes over there!' or 'Shout!' or even 'Now let's hear a diabolical laugh!' And we'd have to do it. When there was anything the instructor didn't like—same thing if anybody tried to get away—you'd get whipped. That hurt. We cried when they whipped us. They even made us build them a road for the trucks that bring in their weapons and provisions. We had to fill in a gully. We had to build a shed to store stuff. Some foreigners came and started asking questions. They were North Americans. They were from the United States. The weapons were from the United States too; we could see that, all you had to do was look.

"I spent two months there. Finally they put us in blue uniforms, gave us guns, and put us in squads that were going to go and fight in Nicaragua. There were 260 of us in all. When we got to Nicaragua, and were about three kilometers inside the border, our buddies in the Nicaraguan army had an ambush set up, and everybody in our group ran. A lot of guys didn't know where to run. The Contras ran for Honduras again. But I stayed there, all by myself, because I wanted to try to escape. And I did. I walked two days and two nights, always scared they might get me again. I got to Totogalpa, and I was sick with nerves. The first nights back home I was sick. I didn't go out anywhere. I felt afraid. Now I'm calm, and when I go to bed I can go to sleep.

"Politics I don't understand. I was just picking coffee to make a little money to live on. They forced me to go with them, they took me against my will, and that's not right. I like working and being free. But the contras force us like that. They told us they were going to win in June, but June's come and gone and they haven't won."

Another kidnap victim I interviewed in Totogalpa is a Delegate of the Word of God who has been working in parish ministry in his community of Santo Domingo for fourteen years. "My name is José Santos López Bautista," he told me, "I'm thirty-two and I'm a farm worker and a Delegate of the Word. I was working on Marcos Tuly's farm, my boss's farm. We started the coffee harvest on November 8, 1983, and we were abducted that same night. Ten guys came to the ranch house with guns and made us line up, forty-two of us, up there to pick coffee. Nobody had any weapons; we were all defenseless. They told us to come with them and that anybody who didn't would be shot. They took us to the border and the next day we crossed over into Honduras, at a place called Las Dificultades. They searched us and took down our names and stuff at a Honduran military post and then they took us to the contra post. Thirty-eight of us got there. Some had escaped along the way. At the camp they had us cut sticks to make lean-tos. The next day thirteen got away. Later others escaped too. So there weren't many of us left, because twenty-four of us had escaped when there were only two contras guarding us, because the ones who'd been out on the kidnapping expedition were really tired when they got back and they slept, but now that they saw that so many had gotten away they started guarding us better.

"I was with them for nineteen days. It was amazing how they said they didn't kidnap. The chief came and he said, 'These have come voluntarily.' But that wasn't true—we'd all been abducted! They insulted the Nicaraguan revolution. They said we're all communists here. They kept telling us about all the aid they get from the United States. The main thing they tell you is that Christians are supposed to be against injustice, and the revolution is unjust, so we should be against the revolution in Nicaragua. They say God's on their side. I saw a kid that got away, but he got lost and they caught him, and they hanged him and quartered him.

"The contras are in communication with the Honduran military there, and one day they got word to get us all out of there quick, because reporters were on the way. So everybody got up and out and headed for the border.

"All the time I was there we went hungry. They hardly ever gave us anything to eat, and when they did it was only rice and potatoes. After a few days they took me with them to Nicaragua, on two missions. I couldn't escape because the chief had heard I'd said something to another guy about running for it, so they really kept an eye on me. But when they took me with them to Nicaragua I didn't know how to shoot. They only taught us how to load and unload, but not how to shoot. They gave us a uniform and a gun, all United States stuff, and sent us into the hills without us knowing how to shoot. The first mission they sent us on was to kidnap some more people. They got three or four people that way. And the other mission was to face off with the Sandinista army, but we didn't meet up with them and anyway that was when I got away. Unfortunately I got lost, in Honduras. I thought I was in Nicaragua and I was in Honduras. It took me four days and four nights to get back to the ranch where I'd been kidnapped. I reported to the authorities and they didn't do anything to me.

"The next year I was clearing some land on Luís Alberto Peralta's farm. I was working there when about twenty contras came along, at five in the morning, and we were abducted. I got away right away. I wasn't going to let them take me this time. But a while later, picking coffee on the same farm, they came at night and took four of us. These were different guys, and there weren't very many of us along this time. If you tried to escape they said you'd be machine-gunned. But I only took it for one night, I took a chance, because by then I knew my way around the mountains. They went into a house. I told them I wanted to get a drink of water, and I went outside. It was night, so it was easy to get away.

"Now this year I'm going back picking coffee again. We're afraid, but we always go, because we have to make a living and because we know that it makes things better for the people. The contras will be back this year kidnapping people. So it's dangerous where we're going, but we can't really do anything about it, scared or not. Recently, just these last few days, they kidnapped some girls up around Dipilto. They're friends of mine and I'm worried about them. We don't know where they are! This has to stop some day, because everything the contras say is a lie. We look at the way things are in Nicaragua and this is where we stay. We organize, we work, and we see the progress the government's made for the people. We only wish the contras would let us live and work in peace!"

SCHOOL BURNED,
ANOTHER *CAMPESINO* ABDUCTED

From Ocotal I went by jeep to Santa María, the closest town to Honduras in the zone; it is only four kilometers from the Honduran border, right up in the mountains. The trip is only a little over fifty kilometers, but it takes over three hours to get there, and nowadays the trip is a real accomplishment, and full of beauty and adventure. The dirt road is incredibly bad and rocky. It winds through endless pine-covered mountains full of passes to Honduras, which can be as near as seven kilometers. This road, with its ups and downs and curves and more curves, affords a view of the mountain ridges, the valleys, and the plains that extend along the Nicaraguan-Honduran border. It's like a no man's land, and so it easily becomes an everybody's land. The few settlements there are at the mercy of the comings and goings of the contras, who have their camps in Honduras; they go back and forth between Honduras and Nicaragua. Viewing this immense territory, one sees how easy it is for the contras to move through the zone along any number of paths or trails into Nicaraguan territory and then return to their camps in Honduras.

The commentary of the priest who drove me there turned the route into a way of the cross. "One night they killed a man and his two sons on that ranch there. . . . Right here is where they ambushed a truck full of people from Santa María and sent it back to Santa María again. . . . This curve is where they stopped Father So-and-So and made him take them the shortest way to Honduras. . . . They shot at a jeep from up there and it fell into that gully. . . . There was a battle here. They took Doña María's thirteen-year-old boy with them. Ran into a patrol here. The fighting started. And they put the kidnappees up front. Doña María's son was killed. His mother's still in mourning. Cries all the time about her 'lost boy.' "

About half-way up the long dirt road through the mountains we came to El Quemazón, a locality where one may contemplate a recent contra "exploit" that seemed to me to be particularly meaningful. The school here, to which children come from a number of settlements and hamlets in the surrounding countryside, is a complex of low, simple, functional buildings, but new, and nice. The school is a symbol of the importance to the Nicaraguan government of literacy and education in poor, remote localities of the Nicaraguan countryside. But on January 24, 1985, a band of contras came through and destroyed a part of the building where materials were kept—reading primers, notebooks, paper, pictures, a map, and the like. They broke down the door, pulled out furniture, and all of the primers, books, notebooks, and paper, and set fire to all of it. The neighbors told me of their fright in seeing the flames. This had happened only ten days before I arrived, and I saw where the bonfire had been—a heap of cinders and black ashes, with bits of paper, notebooks, paperbacks, and primers. It was a beautifully clear symbol of a hatred for literacy, culture, and the education of the poor. During the months before I arrived, the contras had destroyed fourteen village schools and cooperatives in various *campesino* regions of Nicaragua, and had forced 359 schools to close.

Beyond Quemazón, in the little hamlet of El Tizo, I listened to the long story of Lucío Madariaga, who had been taken by the contras three times, only to go free each time. I listened to him next to the clay-walled kitchen of his poor little hut, seated with him and his wife, Isolina, several of his eight children, and a brother. Isolina prepared a pineapple drink. We were going to have lunch. Lucío, Delegate of the Word of God in his community, told his story.

"One day, on my way back from a job sowing corn, I bumped into a group of contras. I was carrying a sack of *maicillo*, and they started searching and questioning me. They had blue uniforms that said 'FDN,' and they had plenty of guns. They already knew I belonged to the local civil defense committee. I had a priest from Spain staying with me at the time, helping me and rooming and boarding with me. They told me they were going to take the so-and-so off with them because he was one of the biggest communists in Nicaragua. The chief asked me what that priest was doing here. I told them he was with me, working in the fields and eating and sleeping with us, and since he was a priest he was able to say Mass for us on the Feast of the Immaculate Conception of Our Blessed Lady. He asked me if it was true that whenever we celebrated the Immaculate Conception novena we'd always close with the Sandinista Hymn. I told him no, that wasn't true, we had novenas to Mary around here the way we'd always had them. Then they said they were going to crush the Sandinista Front, and they offered me money to join them. But I told them no, because I know those guys are the dregs. They showed me the money. They had Nicaraguan money, and they had Honduran *lempiras*. After questioning me and going through my sack they went off in a big hurry. This was January 12, 1983.

"Another time, the same year, I'd just gotten back from Ocotal, and I was lying on my cot taking it easy and strumming my guitar. They came in and pointed their weapons at me. They told me I was 'a goner.' 'Why?' I asked. I told them I hadn't done anything to them. 'We were told to come and get you and get you out of the way,' the chief said. And they took me off. When we got to El Hato they gave me a heavy duffel bag to carry, full of bullets. It said 'USA' on it. I was an adult education coordinator, and that was bad. They told me the money I got from doing that job was 'ill-gotten money.' I told them I didn't get paid anything at all, that wasn't why I was doing it, we did that for the good of the community, for community progress. So they told me again they'd been sent to take me out of there. Then my kids ran up, and a little tiny girl of mine, Fernanda, grabbed them and cried and begged them to let me go. But off we went—then all of a sudden they let me go, in El Hato, and they disappeared. Ever since then my family's uneasy. It's not right. It's a crime to go out persecuting somebody when they aren't doing you any harm, when they're just doing good. The contras won't leave us in peace! That was the second time they took me. That was toward the end of 1983."

Lucío's wife, too, told me that the family lived in fear. She told me the story of the third time the contras had come and taken her husband. Then he told the story:

"The other time was on May 13, 1984. The day before, I was here in my house. That evening a buddy came over from Aguacate and told me the contras were coming. I knew I'd be in for it, and I went over to Santa María. Next day, though, I headed back to Ocotal. We got as far as La Rastra Gorge, where the contras ambushed us. They made us all get out, but I was the only one they took. They gave me a heavy sack of bullets again, with the same lettering on it, 'USA,' and we walked all day till we got to their post in Honduras. We went over that hill near Yure. There were fifty of them, and I was their only prisoner.

"When we got to the post they started questioning me and threatening me. They threatened me with a knife and said they were going to kill me. I told them they could go ahead and kill me, but it was murder, that I hadn't done anything to them and didn't owe them a thing. But then, after they'd threatened to kill me, they started trying to talk me into grabbing a gun and joining them. I told them no, and they laid off, but then they came back and interrogated me and threatened me some more. They had me sitting on a rock. There are no buildings or anything on that post, nothing at all. Prisoners were treated like animals. It was torture. We had to sit out in the rain, nothing to get under at all. They had some old capes. Only the chief had something like a raincoat. He had the radio, so he had this poncho thing to cover him up when he slept. We were freezing. We were starving. Sometimes they'd kill somebody's cow, somebody that supplied them.

"They told me they believed in God, and that down here in Nicaragua the Sandinistas were pure communists and didn't believe in God. And that's why they were going to win, because they believed in God. And they went around with crucifixes. But I always wonder what sort of God they believe in.

"One day they finally decided to take me to La Lodoza, a camp in Honduras where they train people. I wasn't going to go, no siree, not if they were going to take me down there to put me in training or to kill me. And then we got down to the river, the river was high, and we couldn't wade across. We had to use a raft. They sent me over first, then the rifles and ammunition they had. And when I saw that I was all by myself over on the other side, I got away from them. They crossed over, and were after me in a flash. I ran up a hill and dived into a canyon, into a gully. There was a big rock down there with a hole in it like a cave, and I crouched in there. I heard shots. They looked for me for about an hour, but they couldn't find me. 'The so-and-so's gone,' they said, and went back. And there I was, crouched in this cave, just asking God to help me, because if they found me they'd make mincemeat out of me. When it was night, I came out. I started hiking. I found help. The next day I was home. They had me thirteen days. When I got home my wife and kids were desperate. They'd never expected to see me again."

Lucío's wife, Isolina, told me: "When my husband didn't come back and I found out they'd taken him, my heart went out of me. I thought they were going to kill him. For several days I went out looking for him. One day I took my little girl with me, and I just kept asking God to have us meet up with a contra so I could make him give me back my husband. And we did meet up with some. They told me that Lucío was alive. Were we happy! We found out they had him in Honduras. Some contras took me right to the chief who'd taken Lucío. He told me that they were going to let him go, and that he had plenty to eat. And he told me that they were going to help me because of my little girl. Then my daughter said, 'No, Mamá, they already killed Papá, and now you're going to get it yourself—we'd better go back home.' And we went back home."

The Madariagas told me what it was like to live in constant fear: "We're always under threat. They say they're going to come and kill everybody."

Then why did they stay there? Why didn't they leave? Isolina told me that she did want to leave, and that she kept telling her husband so. But Lucío said: "I don't want to leave home. It's not so easy to find a bed and a hut somewhere else when you've got a family this big. We haven't got much, but this is our whole life. Going somewhere else would be like losing our life. We'd never find the little bit we have here anywhere else.

"A good number of people have left from this side of Las Brisas. The contras are threatening us, and they tell us all that if we don't go to Honduras, one way or another they'll come and kill us. People are afraid, and they leave."

SANTA MARÍA, ON THE HONDURAN BORDER

Santa María is perched up high on a mountain; the town is located right on the Honduran border. The first person I interviewed there was a Señor Cástulo López. This was his story of his abduction:

"I was down there in El Arroyo. We were walking along the main road. This was in 1981. I was working for the Field Workers' Association just then. Along came the contras and captured me and tied me up. They took me to where more of them were waiting, twenty-two contras. Once they got me that far, one of them gave me a real whack on the head. He hit me with his rifle. And they took me in the direction of El Encino. When we got there, they threw me down on my back, with my hands tied behind my back, and I had to lie there. They told me they were going to kill me. They told me I might as well say goodbye. They threatened to kill me. They had this knife they were threatening to kill me with. They told me they were going to cut my ear off. Then all of a sudden they took me to a building where they were eating. I was all tied up, see, with my hands behind my back. I couldn't even take a drink of water. One of them gave me a little water to drink, and we headed for the place called El Hato. There were some families from Las Joyas there, and the women were crying. That's where they left me. I guess they just wanted to scare me, because if they'd decided to kill me, they would have. They don't get all tender-hearted all of a sudden."

Next I interviewed a very thin, sprightly, little woman named Jesús López García. I asked her if it was "María Jesús," but no, it was just "Jesús." She told me of the attacks and assaults suffered by the village of Santa María. "Our town goes right up to the Honduran border in the mountains," she said. "Four kilometers in some places. So we live in tremendous tension. We've suffered four attacks in the village. The first time they caught us by surprise. We weren't ready. We had no defense—no shelters for the community, no trenches, no vigilance squad. That was November 8, 1980. Two hundred Guards came up to take the village. They thought they'd win a battle, but they didn't, even though the village was undefended! There were only seven Nicaraguan army fellows, all poorly armed. The contras came storming in behind a hellish rain of bullets, screaming and shouting! We were scared to death. We locked our doors. But they had to retreat. They had to run for it without taking the village. There was one great loss. They killed one of our boys, a great community servant, Hernán Vallecillo. He was a big help in the community. He worked in a craft collective and in a produce collective. He was a driver. And I think he was a Delegate of the Word. The day before, he'd been to a celebration in honor of Carlos Fonseca. The Guards told him this was why he was going to be killed. They hauled him out of his house and cut his throat, not fifteen feet outside the door. He had a little roadside stand, biscuits, things to eat. They stole everything. They took his clothes, left him in his shorts. After they cut his throat they broke his arm!

"The last attack they made here was September 25, 1984. It lasted eight hours. They fired mortars—three mortars at once. They brought in big, heavy weapons. Thank God we were better prepared for civil defense that time. We had our community shelters, and we were organized to defend ourselves. We were inside the shelters, but you could still feel the mortars, rockets, and bombs. What a commotion! The ones on defense were gambling their lives, and thank God only a few places were hit, like one of the high-school classrooms. The high school was built after the triumph of the revolution. The contras also damaged two houses. The blasts killed hens, chicks—even a burro died, at the door of the shelter we were in. They never have been able to take the village, though. We're too united here, thank God! In Somoza's time this was a hotbed of Guards. Somoza built Santa María as a model Somozist showplace. You can see our church bell; it was a gift of Somoza and it's got his name on it. Now we brag that the Guard never has been able to take this village. They attack us, they burn our harvests, they rob us, but we're united here. We defend our sovereignty. Now our defense is our best product! Our other products—well, we've had to let those go sometimes, owing to the attacks by the contras. This place has never been awfully productive anyway. We grow beans, corn, and *maicillo,* enough for ourselves. Now the *campesinos* work the little bit they can, and the people here stay on permanent alert, men, and women too—you can't wander away, because when you remember they've abducted so-and-so, a man, a woman, or a child . . . you can't even remember how many have been kidnapped.

"The contras burn harvests. They burn sacks of beans around here. They steal animals. They steal chickens, hogs, cows, burros, mules, and horses. It won't be long before there aren't any cows left and the kids'll be without milk. People don't like to keep a cow; they'd rather sell it before it's stolen. This war is a great wrong. It's a war of aggression. Those contras are selfish. But the worst thing is the advisers the United States sends. The contras don't think this stuff up themselves; it's actually the United States that gets them to come and commit all these cruelties on us. It looks as if the *Señor Presidente* of the United States doesn't want this little country of Nicaragua to be free! He wants to dominate it himself."

MOZONTE: MORE KIDNAPPINGS

The village of Mozonte, at the foot of the road from Ocotal to Las Manos, has been seized by the contras a number of times. The justice of the peace there, Don Reinaldo Gómez, a Delegate of the Word for eight years, told me about some of the things his family, as well as others, had had happen to them. He himself had been abducted briefly, but he had been frightened more by the kidnapping of his children.

"Yes, it was May 29, 1983. I was at home. I was told my children had been abducted—three daughters, two grown and one in school, and a little boy. My heart sank. They were gone! All I could think of was how to save them. But thank God, they let the two younger ones go and the older ones escaped."

Griselda Gómez, fifteen when I spoke with her, one of the abductees, recounted to me some of the details. "We'd gone out to pick some tomatoes in the garden. That's when the contras came.

They told us to come with them to an old monastery over there in Los Arados. When we got there, there were other people from the valley. They started asking my big sisters questions, and other people too. There were about three hundred of them in blue uniforms. I felt afraid. They passed out a lot of their propaganda sheets. They made us take them and told us we had to read them. The sheets said 'Long live the Pope!' and 'The Pope is on our side!' They had pictures of John Paul II on them, and the contras said, 'Death to Sandinismo' and things like that. They said that the pope was on their side and that they were going to win in Nicaragua with the pope's help. Then they took us to a certain place and they let me and my little brother go. He was nine. They let us go and they took my big sisters with them. And they took other people with them. We went back. We were crying because they had my sisters. But later my sisters got away and came home."

Don Reinaldo also told me the story of the contra attack on the village that occurred at dawn on June 1, 1984. "The battle lasted four hours. There were seven killed." Then there was the mass abduction of 175 civilians—whole families, including women, children, and the elderly. "That was on July 20, 1983. The contras came in firing their weapons and shouting their threats and saying that if we didn't come out they'd toss bombs into the houses. The people came out, terrified. The women and children crying. They lined us up. We filled this street. And they went off with 175 people. They said they were taking them to a meeting."

I later spoke in their home with the Gómezes, a family who had been among the number of the kidnap victims that day. The entire family had been abducted—Don Felipe and Doña Guadalupe and their children. Don Felipe told me: "When we got to a place called El Beneficio de Don Vicente Palacios, the contras said we had to go on ahead. And without telling us where they were taking us, they took us farther and farther, till they got us to Honduras. And after six days in Honduras some Red Cross trucks came and took us to a refugee camp. We were there a year-and-a-half as refugees. We only got back two months ago. About 120 people have come home now." I looked around the room and noticed a home altar along one wall; it had statues of the Blessed Virgin Mary and the saints, and a picture of Bishop Madrigal, the same bishop who, according to one of the abductees, the contras would pray to before going into battle. Bishop Madrigal is buried in Mozonte, where he was a parish priest for many years.

LAS CRUCES:
"CHRISTIANS DON'T KIDNAP AND MURDER"

Las Cruces is a village of 340 Amerindians who live in 40 houses that are somewhat separated. The village spreads along both sides of a road that leads to the Ocotal-Jalapa Highway, and it extends as far as the Coco River, which forms part of the border with Honduras. The large, lovely palm groves at the entrance to the village, the clay, tile-roofed houses surrounded by flowers and trees, the gentle friendliness of its inhabitants—all conspire to give the impression of a little paradise.

The deep traditional piety of the Las Cruces Amerindians is seen in the great crosses of the Way of the Cross that stretches from one end of the community to the other, with the three large ones at the end—Calvary—in a space like a village square. Every year new crosses are erected during Lent. I greeted Don Bernabé, the community patriarch. He had been paralyzed from the waist down by thrombosis for two years, but he was still in charge of the celebration of the Word and community prayer. "They say he's tough, but he's a saint," the priest told me.

The villagers' traditional religious mentality had for years kept the stubborn Indians from taking up arms in their own defense. But on December 7, 1984, at the climax of the community celebration of the most traditional and most deeply rooted religious festival of the Nicaraguan spirit, the Feast of the Immaculate Conception of the Blessed Virgin Mary, the contras subjected the village to a mass kidnapping. And a profound change occurred.

A Las Cruces catechist, José Ortiz, twenty-seven, Don Bernabé's son, told me the story. "We were celebrating the vigil of the Immaculate Conception. The whole community was there for this great feast of Our Lady. Just as the prayers and procession were over, and just as we were sitting down for our traditional coffee, corn liquor, candy, and sugar cane, chatting away, suddenly I saw that the contras had surrounded us and were grabbing some of the kids. I headed out of there as fast as I could. I went into a house, with some kids and some women. The women all stayed by the door so the contras couldn't get in. In no time they were there, and one of them said, 'Let's get these people out of here, they're all in here.' They'd have had us out of there in a minute if the women had let them in. Some guys ran for it, though, and the contras had their reserves out in the street and caught them as they came along. And off they went. There was this big bunch of people out in the street, crying and shouting. The kids were crying because their dads were being taken off somewhere. The operation lasted twenty minutes. They took fifteen of the men of the community. I came out with the others, later, and said, 'The only thing we can do is go sleep up in the hills. Otherwise they might come back and grab us.' And we went up in the hills. Of the fifteen they took, eleven have come back, one has disappeared without a trace, and the other three, as far as we know, were killed by the contras at their camp."

All but one of the abductees who had returned were away for the day, working. Only Mauro Guerrero, eighteen, could have been available for an interview. He had returned wounded. He had run away when he had been sentenced to be executed at dawn. We looked for Mauro a number of times. He seemed to be avoiding us, unwilling to talk about his experience. So I came back to José. The villagers are very open with one another, and well-informed on one another's affairs.

José told me: "Here's what the guys who came back told me. They say that the night of the seventh they were taken to spend the night in El Portillo, about four kilometers from here. The next morning, at about six, they rousted them out and took them to the contras' camp at La Lodoza, in Honduras. They got there about three in the afternoon. They were plenty roughed up in that camp. They had pretty many prisoners there. They told them they were going to train them to come back here and fight communism. The contras claimed they were Christians. That doesn't look much like Christianity to us. The kind of stuff they do isn't the sort of thing Christians do. A real Christian doesn't go around committing all those outrages, as those people do. Real Christians don't kidnap other people the way they do, and mistreat them and murder them the way they do.

"My buddies told me that there wasn't any food in the camp or medical attention or anything. The prisoners got nothing. They said they sent them to wash at night, and that they had to sleep in

wet clothes. When they got back home here they were really wiped
out. They were weak, and their feet were all bloody. Four of them,
the only ones in the militia, had been separated from the others.
They were kept tied up, naked, without anything to eat or drink.
They were beaten something awful, and tortured. Our buddy
Mauro has a wound in his leg that they gave him the night they were
going to kill him. But by the power of God—we in the village had
kept praying to Our Lady and our heavenly Father to lead and
guide them and show them a way to escape—that very night
another of the guys managed to untie him and they both got away.
But in the night they became separated, and to this day we don't
know what happened to the other one. Mauro came along the
mountain trails for five days, wounded, barefoot, and hungry. The
other three must be dead, we figure, because the guys who got away
said they were already starting to kill people, and the prisoners were
digging holes like they were told. Mauro says they took them out at
night two at a time. His turn was at about 3:00 A.M. They jabbed
him in the leg and stomach with a bayonet. His stomach wound was
bad. When he got back here the guys took him to the clinic for
medical attention. He says his buddy was so badly beaten that he
couldn't run as well as Mauro could, and so he couldn't escape.

"That kidnapping was awful for us. And not just for the families, but for the whole community. It was a real blow, an outrage.
We needed those guys. We prayed constantly for their return. We
asked God to help them. And things aren't okay yet—we're still
missing four, even though most have come back. We can see that
what the contras are doing isn't Christian. And so what we've done
is, we've decided to get guns to defend ourselves, so this won't
happen again, so kids won't be without their parents or anyone to
take care of them. Before, the community wasn't armed. We heard
stories, but we didn't believe them; they were too horrible. But then
we saw how the contras came and took our friends and relatives
away. And so we all decided to get guns. Now we can fight! We're
not going to let those people get away with that again, and we're
not going to believe their lies. They go around fooling some people,
saying they're Christians and we're atheists and communists, and
then right while we're praying to the Blessed Virgin, they come and
kidnap us. We're religious; they come to sow terror, hatred, and
revenge among their own people, the Nicaraguan people. We know

them now, and we know how they act and the lies they tell. I don't know if they know what a 'communist' is, but they say we're communists and that's a big lie. They don't fool me. I'm a catechist here, and my family is very religious. I'm getting some kids ready for their First Communion right now, and God willing they'll make their First Communion March 17. We're making plans with our bishop, Bishop Rubén, and the sisters."

When José had finished speaking, there came a small fourteen-year-old, practically a child, swimming in a big militia shirt and wearing a military cap. He carried a small rifle, its barrel covered with paper. I was told that he too had been abducted and taken to the camp, but that he had escaped and come back to the community. His name was Efraím López Blandino. He was too shy to speak to me in front of the adults, and he led me out behind the house. In his adolescent voice, stammering a bit from shyness, he spoke to me.

"It was the Immaculate Conception. The contras came and went off with fifteen of us. They took us to a place they call La Lodoza. We were there several days. It was pretty hard. We were in training. They told us we were going to have to come to Nicaragua to fight. They treated us rough. We'd train all day long, till eight at night. You know, the obstacle-course thing. If you didn't do what you were told, you got dragged in the mud. I saw them stomping on the body of my cousin, trampling his body. They killed others too. All we could think of was how to get back to Nicaragua. They told us to stay with them because Nicaragua was communist. But all we could think of was how to get to Nicaragua. They kept talking to us about religion. But what kind of a religion is that, when you kill guys you've kidnapped? They take them and murder them when they haven't done anything. I was afraid of those guys. I was afraid when they took me, and all the while I was there I was afraid. I was also afraid they were going to send me to Nicaragua to fight. I didn't want to. I was afraid all the time. I didn't cry, but I shook. Then I got away. There were five of us. We hiked for a long time. We were really tired when we got back. All along the way we only had guinea bananas to eat, and guinea *cojoyotes*. Once I got back I decided to join the militia, so they couldn't take me away like that again."

I said goodbye to Efraím and stopped in one more time at

Mauro's. He'd been in and out. Mistrustfulness, fear, shock? I thought: they had tortured him, he knew that they intended to kill him, that he was going to die within a few hours; then his friend, another kidnap victim, untied him, and he escaped death; but in his flight he lost that friend. What sort of scars does that leave on an eighteen-year-old boy?

I moved closer to Ocotal and visited another Amerindian, Martín Vanegas Pérez, thirty-six, whose wife—Francisca Sánchez de Vanegas, thirty-four—had been kidnapped, along with their three children. "We were living in El Cambalache, near Las Manos. It was December 5, a Sunday. I'd gone to Ocotal to see somebody. I came back the next day, Monday. They'd kidnapped everybody, my wife and the kids. They'd told her either she went along or she'd have her throat cut. To save her life she'd gone to Honduras with them. They took the kids too. She begged them to let them go, day and night she begged them. Finally they let her go, but they told her that if she went back to Nicaragua they'd kill her within twenty-four hours. She stayed in Honduras a whole year, working, waiting for a chance to come back. I never had any news of her till the day I saw her back with the kids. I'd figured they were dead. The contras—if they were human, like we're made to the image of God, they wouldn't do those things."

I thought about the Las Cruces community for a long time that night. The Amerindians of Las Cruces would not be armed today had the contra forces not outraged them with their "big haul" on the Vigil of the Immaculate Conception. And then telling the abductees that they, the abductors, were "Christians"! But they did it, and that was what had motivated the village to arm.

SANTA ROSA: EXPERIMENT IN COMMUNITY

An interesting experiment that was begun in June 1983 is being brought to completion by thirty Amerindian *campesino* families in an area near Ocotal. Faced with the insecurity and fear occasioned by the contras' kidnappings and murders, they have taken up a collective, group approach to community life, in education, housing, production, and defense.

I visited their community, their settlement, in Santa Rosa. You leave the road leading from Ocotal to Jalapa and head into the bush. You go through hills and grazing land while traveling in the direction of the Coco River. All the members of the community live together under the high-arching ceiling of an old ranch house or in huts and native houses of stakes and straw while they build their new homes and community buildings.

I interviewed José, a member of the militia. José sat cleaning his rifle. He was surrounded by other members of the militia, two ladies, numerous children, and hens and chicks. In the farmyard were calves. "There are thirty families here," he told me, "two hundred people. We used to live in Limón Valley, in El Caracol, El Zarzal, and El Varillal, and along the Amucayán Valley of Telpaneca. We were scattered. There was always the danger the contras might come along and make off with somebody. Now we're all together, so we can work in an organized way and so there'll be less danger. We got together in this old ranch house here in Santa Rosa in June 1983. We're using it till we finish building our own community housing."

With brick, wood, and cement, the people are building fifty homes and a large child development center on some graded terrain along the valley. On several of the hills I could see watchtowers. The only trouble is the contras. "We're right on their route," José told me. "We're organized for defense, and we have our sentry posts. We're always on the watch. They've been down this way, but we've spotted them and they've had to change plans."

On the wall of the ranch house I observed posters honoring those murdered by the contras: José Pío Gutiérrez, Delegate of the Word of God in Limón Valley: "He was out looking for an uncle who'd been kidnapped. He was very worried about him. They caught him on the road and killed him on the spot." Andrés Ruiz López: "It was December 9, 1983. He'd gone down to the Coco River. They caught him and killed him. We went looking for him, and days later we found his body." Hermógenes Pastrana: "Another Delegate of the Word, killed July 31, 1984."

José concluded: "Here we're organized in committees for work, defense, child and adult education, and production. We grow first-rate beans, and then corn, tomatoes, vegetables, cabbages, and onions. And we have livestock—we've been eating veal and we're starting to get cow's milk. We're making progress here. Without the contras we'd do better. We'd have happier lives."

THE ENDLESS ANGUISH . . .

In the town of Ocotal I interviewed Doña Cecilia Castellanos, a widow from Santa María. She spoke to me of the loss of her son, who had been abducted by the contras. She also related to me an account of a very recent kidnapping—of which she had been the eyewitness—that had taken place on the premises of a private coffee grower.

"First they took my son Carlos from me. He was so young, only twenty-one. He was still studying, but he was already working as a law assistant in a village court. He'd just gotten married. It was June 10, 1983. He was on his way from Dipilto with his cousin, my nephew Trino, who lived in Jalapa and worked as an adult education assistant. They were coming along the road and were ambushed. It was when they were blowing up the bridge. They took several of our people. They've never been heard from. It'll be two years in June. I feel as if it were the first day. I have such great sorrow and pain. I can't talk about it any more."

Tears rolled down her dark, Amerindian face. "We've suffered so much because of the contras. Here in the house there's no man to help. Carlos helped me. Now my daughter and I are alone because the contras killed her husband too, recently, in an ambush in San Juan de Limay. He left two children and a pregnant wife. Now I depend on my elder son, Manuel. He's a high-school teacher. The contras are always threatening teachers. Many, many of the teachers live here in Ocotal.

"The other thing that happened to me was last Tuesday, a week ago yesterday. We were on Don Basilio's coffee farm. We'd finished the coffee measuring for the day. We were sitting there talking, waiting for the truck, because they were going to pick us up at four in the afternoon and take us back—nobody wanted to stay and sleep on the farm, the contras might come. Right then, when we were talking, I heard somebody say, 'Up with 'em there, nobody move. You're surrounded.' All I said was, 'Holy Jesus, be thou with us now!' I lost my mind. But in a minute I thought of the kids. I had my two little kids with me. Jimmy was on a bridge. I went right over and got him. The little girl had seen the contras and had gone and hidden in some guinea bushes. There she was, hiding somewhere in there, and me running around the bushes calling her. Then there was this bunch of kids crying and people shouting. And the contras rounding us up. Suddenly my little girl came out of the bushes as fast as her little legs could carry her and jumped up in my arms shouting, 'Mommy, Mommy!' So now I had them both, and I held them so close. Then I felt courage come into me. From that moment on I had no fear. I had courage. I thought, 'Well, if I die, it's all right.'

"So they had us rounded up, and off we went. I was in a group with my brother Julio, a gentleman of fifty-two. They wanted to take him along, but he wouldn't budge. They kept coming up and saying, 'Move!' but he said no, he wasn't going anywhere. I told him, 'Julio, look, let's go, let's get in line! Only God can help us now!' And he went. We went over a little bridge and lined up with the people they had that they were going to abduct. I had my arms around my two kids. The little girl was crying, so was the boy. One of the contras got mad because the kids were crying. I turned around to them and I said, 'Haven't you got a Christian bone in your bodies? Don't you know kids cry? What good is it going to do you to take these kids?' They told me the chief said they had to. And they said, 'If you're afraid, what do you go out picking coffee for? You're only picking coffee so you can buy weapons. Don't think you're going to bring in the harvest!' I said, 'We do it because we have to earn a living.'

"The line of civilians was in front; the contras were behind us. A lady in front of me was crying because they were taking her kids along; they were twelve or thirteen years old or so. Several ladies were crying because they had kids with them. Then the contras said that ladies with kids could go back. I got right out of there. There were lots of us with kids along. And my brother, who didn't want to go with them anyway, see, joined our group! 'No you don't!' said one of the contras, and all us women and children hunched over and put our arms over our heads. We thought they were going to kill us and all the kids. We figured they were going to kill us for sure. I got between Julio and the contra and said, 'Get going, Julio! Don't go back!' And we made it, with Julio with us. We got up the slope and down the other side, out of sight.

"I don't know how many people they took. Seemed as if they'd gone around getting different people from different places. Before they let the women and children go, there were about forty of us all told. The contras had blue uniforms on. They had big, heavy guns. I hate all this. I was sick a lot, from fright. I spent all day yesterday depressed."

There were many stories like Doña Cecilia's. The contras do their kidnapping on the ranches within their reach during the coffee harvest, from December to March. Besides simply making off with people, they try to disrupt the coffee harvest. Coffee is Nicaragua's main export, and they hope to strike a blow against the economy of the country. But they hurt the private producers too, the individual landowners of the coffee ranches. And they do a great deal of further damage to the *campesinos* and working families, who obtain the bulk of their annual income from the coffee harvest. The field workers are terrified by the kidnappings, abuse, and murders. The brutal murder in Honduras of Felipe and María Barreda, the couple who worked for the church and were kidnapped in 1983 during the coffee harvest in this part of the country, is fresh in their memory.

A private coffee grower from Ocotal told me: "I'm in trouble in my business as a result of the kidnappings on our coffee farms. This week they took some harvest workers from another private farm near my property and there was panic. It's been like this for several years. I don't have enough workers—I need a hundred and thirty and I've got fifteen. The people around here are terrorized by the incursions onto the farms. They're afraid, and they don't go out picking even though they need to in order to earn a living. These attacks hurt my production. They take the harvesters to Honduras. My production is down. The coffee is falling off the bushes. I've worked this farm, hard, for fifteen years. I have six children, and I might not be able to keep sending them to school. I don't think they consider me an enemy. I'm a private producer and I don't get mixed up in politics. In fact I'm conservative! I belong to the Conservative Party and I was educated in the United States."

I witnessed the departure from Estelí of a number of truckloads of volunteers for the coffee harvest in the north of Nicaragua. It was dramatic. It was as if they were being sent off to war. With courage like this, the people were actually bringing in a good percentage of the coffee harvest for the 1984–85 season.

THE RAPE OF TWO *CAMPESINAS*

I also interviewed two women, two young mothers, in Ocotal. They seemed to be very poor, and I could see that they were extremely frightened. They told me their names—Adelina and Josefa Inestrosa—and, after some hesitation, their ages. They were twenty and twenty-two. I would have said they were older. Trembling and tearful, while their children whimpered and whined, they told me their story.

Adelina began. "We were home with our mom, who was sick, and our kids. We lived in a little house on a bit of land we'd been lent by one of the coordinators; the house was in Susucayán, in El Jícaro. One night around Christmas, about ten o'clock, six contras came in and turned out the lights on us. They were looking for my brother. They told us that if we didn't hand him over they'd kill us. We told them he wasn't there, which was true. He was in San Nicolás. They told us they were going to wait for him a week. But they only stayed two hours. They left the same night. They beat us, hit us in the chest, and then raped us. Both of us. Two contras raped each one of us. We didn't know them and we couldn't see them because they'd turned out the lights on us. They had flashlights and they turned them on when they wanted to find us and scare us."

Josefa went on: "We were in one room. The house has only one room. My mom, who's sick, was there, and so were all the kids. The kids were crying. They'd tied me to one of them, Manuel de Jesús, but he got loose. They looked for him, but they couldn't find him, the lights were off. They'd just turn their flashlights on and off. My daughter hid in a pile of sacks of corn. Another girl ran out back. They came to me and hit me, three times, with a rifle. It knocked the breath out of me, and I bent double. After they did that they raped me. Two contras raped me. Then they raped my sister. They didn't touch my mother, we told them she was very sick, and they told her to wait, they'd see that she got an operation, everything was going to be better after they'd won. They told the kids not to cry. The kids were scared, and crying. They told them they'd help us later."

Adelina: "After they threatened and hit us and raped us in front

of my mom and the kids, before they left they threatened us again.
They told us that they were going to be right close by and that they
were coming back. They said the house was surrounded by contras."

Josefa: "We didn't sleep that night. We thought they were going
to come back and kill us. First thing next morning we ran away. We
left the house, we left everything, and came running to Ocotal to
find a relative. It took us four hours. We still don't dare go home
after what they did to us."

The young women were terrified and lost. Fear glistened in their
large, bright eyes as they gazed at me unblinkingly, shedding silent
tears. Their skin was dark. They were thin. They wore their hair in a
bun. They trembled. They made me think of frightened gazelles.
Two dislocated, ruined lives. They walked with a quick, nervous
step, their children clinging to their dresses. I couldn't get over their
total poverty and helplessness. Even more than their bodies, their
lives had been raped.

THE RAPE OF TWO WEST GERMANS

After speaking with Adelina and Josefa, I made a trip to Santa
María. On my return to Ocotal I read in the paper that the contras
had raped two women from West Germany, near Pantasma. That
night I kept seeing those terrified, tearful eyes, the eyes of Adelina
and Josefa. Several days later, on my return to Managua, I located
the young German women who had been raped. They asked to
remain anonymous but told me the facts, "so that the world will
know what the contras are doing and what U.S. policy is doing
when it supports the contras. The United States is guilty of this
dirty war because it's aiding and abetting it." In halting but under-
standable Spanish, with occasional help from a dictionary or a
gesture, they told their story.

"We're from the Federal Republic of Germany. We belong to the
team of Germans doing housing construction in Loma Alta, in
Pantasma Valley, for a coffee co-op. This team of ours has been
working in Nicaragua for a year. One group works two months and
then another group comes and continues. There are twenty of us in
each group. When we get back to Germany we work for solidarity
with Nicaragua and the other peoples of Central America. We

collect money and send aid. We bring money to buy construction materials and tools. We want to give this help to the needy peoples of Central America."

The other woman continued: "We've built twenty-eight houses. *Campesinos* who used to live in El Ventarrón, and were attacked by the contras three times, are already living in them. The last time they were attacked, in May 1984, three hundred Guards destroyed their whole co-op. Last September a woman was kidnapped from the co-op by the contras and hasn't been heard from since."

The first young woman: "Now we're building roads, digging wells, setting up toilets. We plan to build a community center, a health station, and thirty more houses. We're going to keep at it. Money comes from Germany, from the solidarity groups there. This is volunteer work. We pay our own expenses—travel, room, and board."

The second: "Now listen to what the contras did to us. On February 2, 1985, the two of us left Jinotega, at about 6:00 A.M., for Pantasma, in a public bus on its regular route. We were the only Germans. There were about twenty Nicaraguans. It was public transport. We'd gone to Jinotega the day before because she—this one—had cut her finger on the job."

The first: "After about two hours on the road, the bus stopped to let some people off. And just as we were starting out again a man came out from behind a house and whistled. The bus stopped again and the man came up with a revolver. He pointed to the two of us and said, 'You get out.' And he told the driver to keep going.

"This man asked us what we were doing in Nicaragua. Four other men came out of the field or woods onto the road. Two of them had revolvers, and all of them carried hand grenades. They took us into the woods. They searched our bags and our clothes looking for weapons. We saw that two of these men had been in the bus with us on the trip from Jinotega. They kept asking us what country we were from. We said we were from the Federal Republic of Germany. And they saw our passports. But they saw our Cuban Airlines stamp, too, and they said we were Cubans and must be teachers or nurses!"

The second young woman continued: "They were very annoyed that we did not understand Spanish well and that she kept saying things to me in German. They had a discussion among themselves, then they made us hike about fifteen minutes into the wood toward the hills. Then four other men came, also carrying hand grenades. Some of the first five left, but the leader stayed. When we got to a certain place, near a field, they separated us and raped us. The chief and another took turns raping us—each of them raped us both."

The first: "While the second contra was raping me, the chief was telling me I had better pay attention to what he was going to say. And he told me that he and the other one were soldiers of the Nicaraguan Democratic Force and that they were allies of Edén Pastora's contras. And he said that he himself had received his training in the United States, on an army post. He told me that he thought we must be from some country that was helping the Sandinistas, and so we were enemies of the contras' struggle. I told him that our country was West Germany, and so our government certainly wasn't helping the Sandinistas, that it had cut off aid and was helping the contras directly or indirectly with weapons and money. He tried to convince us that the contras were good people, 'better than the Sandinistas.' He insisted I was Cuban. He said he was going to abduct us to Honduras to train us to fight alongside the contras. He said he ran a company of two hundred men in the hills and showed me his commission. I think one of his last names was Rodríguez. He finally realized that I wasn't going to have anything to do with him and wouldn't even look at him. He said that the contras didn't want foreigners in their country and we'd better go back to Germany and put in a good word for the contras."

The second: "After he raped me the chief told me he didn't kill women, that only the Sandinistas kill women. And he wanted to have this medal here around my neck to remember me by. I told him no, and he could see I meant it. Then he put his revolver to my head."

The first: "We could see that they were paid by the United States and trained by the United States. There are some confused, duped *campesinos* with them, but they're not the ones who are the enemy. It's the contras and the United States that are persecuting the Nicaraguan people."

3

Estelí:
The Massacres

The accounts and testimony I heard in Estelí, capital of the department of Estelí, seventy kilometers from Ocotal and 150 from Managua, reminded me of the massacre of San Francisco del Norte, one of the first to rouse the indignation of Nicaragua. From 1982 to 1984 the bloody slaughter included ambushes of the civilian population. Survivors of the new massacres, which had occured in various localities in the departments of Estelí and Jinotega during those years, like the survivors of the San Francisco massacre, spoke of blood, death, and terror suffered by their families, neighbors, and co-workers whenever the contras came.

A WEDDING PARTY

In Estelí I interviewed Orlando Palacios Ramos, an emaciated, fifty-two-year-old *campesino*, the father of six children. We spoke for two hours. Behind his lively words and gestures I viewed a bloody tragedy.

"It was December 24, 1984. My son and his girlfriend had celebrated their wedding at 6 P.M. in Wiwilí. That's where she's from, Wiwilí, and my son works there. After the wedding we started over to the reception, all peppy and having fun. It was a quiet night, and we spent the next day getting rid of a hangover as usual—or I did anyway. Couple too many the night before. Then that evening we got up to take the bus back home, but the bus didn't come. My wife and I wanted to come home that day, the twenty-fifth, but I told her, 'Look, the bus isn't coming; we're going to have to stay here. There's no other way to get there.' But one of the guys I'd been drinking with said, 'I've got a truck. I'll take you straight to Jinotega. At five tomorrow morning we head for Jinotega.'

"So, fine, that night I went to bed pickled again—if you'll pardon my language. My wife put me to bed. When I woke up, after midnight, I said, 'Where are we?' My wife said, 'We're where we stayed for the wedding, with our son's girlfriend's aunt. They got married.' 'Who else is here?' I asked. 'Doña Yolanda, the lady who came from Managua. She came for the wedding and for three little girls she has here. We're all leaving tomorrow morning.' 'Look, sweetheart,' I said, 'that's all fine, but you know I'm not crazy about traveling in the wee hours of the morning like that.' 'I'm not either, darling,' she said, 'but the guy with the truck told us to be there at five sharp!'

"Must've gotten to be about three by the time we were done talking. Then my wife told me, 'Get up and wash. I'm going to wash up too.' 'Who feels like washing up?' I told her. 'If you'd brought along a pint I'd down a swig or two and I'd feel like washing up. I'll just go as I am, I want to go back to sleep. Besides, I don't want to go out in the dark.' 'I don't either,' she said. But everybody got up and washed. My wife washed up, and then I hear the water running again in the bathroom and I asked, 'Who's in there?' My new daughter-in-law answered me. 'Great,' I said to myself, 'let her wash up, she's a young girl and doesn't feel the cold. Me, I'm old and hung over and I feel the cold. I'm not going to wash up.'

"So everybody got washed, and then we heard the truck honking for us to make it snappy. We got in and started off. There were ten of us—four men and six women: my son, his wife, my wife, Doña Yolanda and her three daughters, the driver, me, and an adjutant who was going home.

"Just after we got beyond the village I got sick to my stomach. I was hung over and we were riding in the dark. I threw up. Then I sat down on the spare tire. We were all sitting down. I had my wife on one side of me and one of the girls on the other. I said to my wife,

'Why don't you let me have the money I had?' 'Because I don't want you drinking,' she said. 'All right then,' I said, 'when we stop at the levee, money or not, I'm going to down a couple. Doña Yolanda here'll lend me some money won't you, Doña Yolanda?' 'Sure,' said Doña Yolanda.

"So we're riding along, having a peaceful, enjoyable conversation. Just after crossing the river, we notice a bridge that's been damaged by the contras. 'Look at that bridge!' I yelled. Somebody else said, 'Sure, but you can cross it, they couldn't bring it down.' So we're riding along nice and peaceful. Then about a kilometer up ahead a woman with two boys stops us. The kids are, say, twelve or thirteen. She asks us to take her to Pantasma, says she had to spend the night where she was because there wasn't a bus to Pantasma. The driver doesn't want to take her because it's an inconvenience; it's a detour and we want to go straight to Jinotega. So the driver says, 'I'm not taking her.' We haven't gone two kilometers from there when we felt an explosion and hear a lot of shots. The truck rattles and shakes, and I grab my wife and the girl and pull them down on my lap and lean down over them. 'Hit the floor!' I say. 'The contras are trying to kill us!' And I push them down onto the floor of the truck and lie down between them. And we feel the chill of death. We can only cry to God, 'God, Three in One, Divine Child, what is happening to us, Divine Child?'

"Once the mine has exploded the truck stops dead. But the driver starts it up again and pulls it off the road. So the mine hasn't blown up the truck. So that's over, but I stay stretched out between my wife and the girl. Over on the other side is the fat lady, Doña Yolanda, and the two other girls. Then there's the adjutant, and in front are the driver, my son, and his wife. After the mine, I think that'll be all there is to it, but then they start in on us with rifle fire, crack, crack, crack! The only other thing I can hear is our people crying. I'm lying down, and I don't let my wife or the girl up. The spare tire's by my head. But that hail of bullets! Then hand grenades. I don't pass out, I only scream. I don't try to make it out of the truck, I only wait for death. Then I feel this first shot, in the arm. I say to my wife, 'Mama, we're going to die for sure, but don't you mind!' The grenades keep exploding, and our people keep screaming, between the blasts, 'Don't kill us, we're civilians!' They keep shooting. And I hear my wife say, 'Divine Child, save us!' No sooner does she say this than she gets a bullet in the back. I'm holding her in my arms. She just lifts her head up once, then she sinks back down on my shoulder. 'Sweetheart, they've killed me.' I tell her, 'But don't you mind, precious, because I'm shot too.' That's when I feel this shot that grazes my forehead, though it doesn't hurt. 'Precious, we're going together. God wants us, don't you mind, we're going to die right together,' I tell her. She never speaks another word.

"After that I just listen to the shooting, but I've got this shot in my side. Our people are just screaming, the women are thrashing and writhing. I hear another voice: 'Don't shoot! They're civilians!' Then the shooting stops, and I see some people come up to the truck. Four come up. I can't make them out very well, because the grenades and explosions have sort of blinded this eye, but I see them come up after the shooting is over. I grab the railing inside the truck and pull myself up. I look at them with my good eye and shout at them—I'm really mad—'Look what you've done! What do you think you're doing? There aren't any weapons here! You haven't even killed any men, you've killed just women, just girls, you've just murdered little girls!' So I'm on one side of the truck and I look at all the dead girls. The four guys don't say a thing. They just motion with their heads, turn around, and leave.

"They were contras, I identified them as that for sure, I know their weapons, they'd kidnapped me three times. There were four of them that came up to the truck, but there were more. There were two more in front of the truck, and they left too. They left together. They were in olive drab. And that's an open place, flat, a plum orchard. It's called Zompopera. It was a clear day, and it was 6:00 A.M. Our truck couldn't have been confused with any military vehicle. It was a red Nissan! It's incredible, but they're murdering the people, they're killing civilians. This is murder! They're not trying to liberate the country, they're trying to murder it!

"So they went away. I was wounded. I looked at my dead wife, and I decided to crawl along the bed of the truck as best I could and drop down on the road and try to get up again and get to the cab to see if my son was dead too. I figured he was dead. I got to the cab and poked my son in the back. He was leaning against the door, half conscious. I pulled at his head. I said, 'Boy, are you dead?' 'No, dad,' he said, 'I'm still alive.' 'What about the driver?' I hoped that the truck would get us out of there. 'The driver's been dead a while.' 'And your wife?' 'She's dying. Dad, how are *you*?' 'I've been shot, but I'll live.' 'What about mom?' 'Your mom died in my arms. But don't you mind, she didn't suffer. She died in my arms—that's why I came up to see if you were dead, so I could cry some more,' I told him, 'since that's the only thing an unarmed person can do—cry more.' 'I'm shot,' he told me, 'but I'm alive.' I'll help you get out of there,' I said. He was trapped. Then I grabbed onto him the best I could, I pulled his arm here like this, I pushed the driver off him, then I pushed the bride off of him. And I got him out. And we started talking, down on the road. His girl was crying. She was dying. He couldn't take his eyes off her.

"At this point, I said to my son, 'Look, boy, your mom is dead, they're all dead, I don't know if the adjutant is alive or not. The only thing I can do is go down this road and see if there's anybody who'll help us, good people.' I got up and left. I dragged myself about a kilometer. Everything looked fuzzy. I came to a hut. There were three men there. When they saw me all bloody they were scared, but I said, 'Don't be afraid,' and I asked the people there to help us. They took me to a ranch called Los Ubeda, that they call 'the Twins.' They gave me coffee. I had this terrific thirst. I asked for black coffee, I didn't want any water. I lay down on a workbench. People came and I told them what was going on. And I said, 'Help the survivors! The dead you can forget because they're dead. Just rescue the survivors, that's all. Even my wife's dead there, Doña Yolanda's dead, her girls are all dead, everybody's dead. When I left there were three people alive, my son, his wife who was dying, and the adjutant, who's at least got a couple of broken legs. If those three are alive, get them out of there, so they won't be in a heap of corpses!' Then a boy came along on a horse. He went galloping off, and when he came back he said, 'There's almost nobody left. They're all dead except your son, he's alive, and one girl who's dying. I'll go get a stretcher and find some people to carry her away on the stretcher.'

"So that's what happened. They finally came with the girl—my son's wife, who was dying—on the stretcher, with my boy limping along with them. He'd been shot in three places. The ambush was about 6:30 A.M. The conversation I'm telling you about started around eleven. We started for the hospital about 3:00 P.M. and got there an hour later. They took seven bodies out of the truck—five female and two male, the adjutant and the driver. Of the five females, two were grown women and three were children— Yolanda's daughters, twelve, thirteen, and fourteen years old. Only my son and I survived."

Orlando finished his story. He was exhausted, drained. But he kept insisting—without gestures now, his head between his hands—"They're murdering the people. They're not liberating them, they're murdering them. I lived to tell the tale. I should have been murdered, but God placed his hand on me so I could tell this, so it can become history—so the world will know what kind of murderers they are."

FARM WORKERS

"It was a massacre," three survivors had told me, in Ocotal. A truck carrying thirty civilian farm workers was ambushed, bombed, and burned, by 150 contras, in El Pericón, department of Madriz, north of Estelí. The workers had been on their way to pick coffee. The 1984 harvest, which eventually was brought to a successful conclusion, began in blood and fire.

In Ocotal I first interviewed a wounded survivor. Carlos's face was swollen with the wound from a bullet that had entered the top of his head and had come out the tip of his chin. He had lost his vision in one eye, and his mouth twisted when he spoke. "We were riding along in the truck, about thirty of us. We'd gotten as far as Pericón when we heard the first shots and rocket blasts. I dived for the side of the bed of the truck, trying to protect myself. I didn't know it, but they'd got me, and I just lay there along the edge of the truck bed. Some of our people were groaning. One girl grabbed me and told me not to leave her, she'd been hit. But I threw myself out of the truck, rolled a few meters, and jumped into the brush along the edge of the road, right when the truck came to a halt."

A few days later in Estelí I met two more wounded survivors, Jorge Luís Briones and his brother Santos Róger. Róger, who had the face, voice, and shyness of an adolescent, told me: "I don't work in Telcor. I'm in school. I've finished my elementary education. I wanted to go and pick coffee to help the country's economy a bit. So I joined my brother's brigade of Telcor workers to go pick coffee. He was the chief. I wanted to go in a group."

He spoke slowly, with great concentration, and sometimes with such emotion that he would perspire and his voice would break off. Here is the story Santos told.

"There were thirty-five of us. It was a Tuesday, December 4, 1984. At 7:45 A.M. we got into the truck to go pick coffee in La Dalia, in San Juan, on the Coco River. Ten minutes later, as we passed through El Pericón, we were ambushed. A small truck with some armed civilians was ahead of us, to protect us while we were picking, and they let that truck through. They opened fire on our truck, though, with machine guns, LAU RPG-7 rocket launchers, and rifles. The truck kept going about another three hundred meters until a rocket blew out its tires and it went down a ravine. It was still right-side-up, but some of our people were already dead. Others were still alive, but some of those were wounded. I'd been riding on the knapsacks, lying down, with my feet up, like this. I got hit in the foot. The first bodies fell on top of me and got blood all over my clothes and my face. I got out of the truck somehow and dragged myself along a few meters. Then I played dead. Then the contras came up to the truck and cut anybody's throat that was screaming. Then they set fire to the truck, with some people still alive in it, including a mother and her little kid, five years old, that we were giving a ride to."

Róger was tense, and there were moments of silence as he struggled to control his emotion. He went on: "They thought I was dead. I was just lying there on the road, all bloody. A contra came up and pulled my boots off, and took them with him. Then another one came up and took my socks. Then others came up and searched my pockets to see if I had any money. But they didn't find any. One of them said, 'This sonofabitch is broke!' They went through our pockets, everybody's, even the corpses'. They took the knapsacks, they took everything, before they set fire to the truck with the wounded inside.

"Just a couple of meters from where I was lying was one of the guys with both his legs shot up; he was moaning. As they went by him they slit his throat with a bayonet and then they machine-gunned him. I saw them slit some wounded people's throats if they'd jumped out of the truck, and then they machine-gunned them. And then I heard the screams of the wounded ones inside as they were burning alive.

"When they'd set fire to the truck, they left. Then I saw one of our guys, who was wounded, get into the truck and pull somebody out, but one was all he could get out, because the truck was engulfed in flames. The contras must've been scared, because I heard them say, 'Let's get outa here, before we get caught!' The whole thing took less than an hour."

In Róger's bright eyes I could see him relive the scene he was describing. He was perspiring. "I couldn't get out of there. My foot was shot up. The whole thing was all cramped up and it had these fragments in it." And he showed me his foot, with the stitches in his big toe, and the scars on his leg. "About two o'clock the army came and went after the contras. They took me to the health station in Telpaneca and then transferred me to Somoto in an ambulance."

I asked Róger what he thought while all this was going on. Was he afraid? Did he think he was going to die? Very close to tears, he told me: "I wasn't afraid. I was mad. It might've been hate or something like that. I didn't wonder whether I was going to die or not. I just said, 'God's will be done.' I wasn't praying. I was just thinking about God. And I felt wild anger at those guys that were doing all that to innocent people. Now I feel real bad. I feel very bad, and I feel more determined to defend my people and their revolution."

Jorge Luís Briones, twenty-six, had recovered from his wounds and spoke with me calmly, with an emotion that had crystallized into resolve. "There were five women along, there was my brother, there were two more kids like him, and the rest of us were Telcor workers. I was brigade chief. A brigade is what we call a group of volunteers going out together to pick coffee. We were on our way up to the coffee plantations. Most of us were traveling in this dump truck. Most in the truck were unarmed. Five or six of us or so—we knew how the contras had perpetrated massacres on our civilian population and had kidnapped them from the coffee harvest—five or six of us had volunteered to carry guns in case it'd be necessary to defend the guys and the women.

So there we were, riding along in the truck, joking and having a good time, laughing, on our way to pick coffee. I was riding in the cab with the driver. In the back were the women, my brother, and all the others. Practically all of them were unarmed. We got as far as a community they call El Pericón. We'd climbed a hill. It was a winding road. We didn't know it, but there was a column of contras along the edge of the road. We didn't see them. We knew we were in an ambush only when they started shooting. They launched rockets, threw grenades, machine-gunned us with sixties, and shot at us with rifles, right from the roadside. I jumped out of the truck, bullets flying all around me, hit the dirt, and rolled down a little grade. I got up. I'd been hit in the leg. I still had my rifle and my equipment. I remembered the women. There was a woman in the truck with a five-year-old boy. She'd asked us for a ride. I remembered the little boy, I remembered the women, I remembered all those unarmed people. I remembered my brother. I remembered all those massacres the contras had committed. And the love I felt for those people riding with me got stronger than the pain I felt in my leg. I managed to climb back up to the road, and there was a group of contras moving toward the truck, firing their rifles. Nobody was shooting from the truck. There were only wounded and dead in the truck. I managed to get off a few shots. We exchanged fire. For about fifteen minutes I held them off. Lots of people in the truck were dead. Now there were only unarmed wounded guys and women crying in there. There was no resistance from the truck, which was about a hundred meters from where I was shooting. I got hit in the hand. Then I got hit in the head by a bullet that almost knocked me unconscious. That was a really bloody wound."

Jorge showed me the scar of that wound, on the left side of his head, near the temple. He also showed me the other wound, from the bullet in the leg.

"I saw it'd be crazy to try to keep holding them off like that. So I rolled a little farther down the grade. The contras tried to follow me, but I still had hold of my rifle and I kept shooting, so they turned around and ran for the truck, to finish their job, finish massacring the unarmed guys and women. By now I'd been hit in the leg, head, and hand. I managed to hide in some brush, and from there I could see some of the atrocities the contras committed on the wounded, some of them only slightly wounded, say, with a broken leg from a bullet. I was so weak I just watched, sort of without thinking of anything. I saw that there were women crying up there, and there was a kid who was crying too. So they tossed grenades into the truck to finish off anybody still alive in there. I saw how the contras would go up to fallen bodies and run them through with their bayonets to finish them off. Then I saw how they started to burn the truck, after they took the knapsacks, clothes, shoes, everything, even off the corpses.

"I felt angry. But I couldn't move. And I was just about out of ammo. I had about ten cartridges left. From where I was I could see how they burned the truck. They set fire to the truck even though after all their grenades there were still people screaming in there. They set fire to it without a second thought. Then they ran off.

"After that I could only watch my buddies' bodies catching fire, and some that were along the roadside. I saw a girl trying to jump out of the truck when the contras were still there and one of them opening up on her with his machine gun, point blank. He practically emptied his FAL on her.

"When they ran for it, they passed only a few meters from me. They were really moving. Then I passed out and that was the last thing I knew. When I came to again, I tried to get back up to the road to see what'd happened, but I slipped and fell and passed out again. By the time I actually got up there it was pretty late. Nobody was there but an army contingent. They'd collected the bodies, all charred, and a couple of wounded survivors, who'd hidden, like me. Six or eight or so survived. About twenty-five bodies. They sent me to the hospital. They told me my brother was dead, but we met in the hospital."

I asked Jorge for more details of what he had seen and heard. He told me: "During the firefight, all I could see were about thirty contras, but afterwards, when they went right by me, I could see that there were, oh, about 150 or 180 of them. When they were robbing the truck, taking everything they could lay their hands on, I could hear them laughing and joking about our people, and hooting and hollering about all the 'good stuff' they were finding—boots, blankets, and clothes they were stealing from the bodies. Most of the weapons they had, at least the rocket launchers, were from the United States, I'm sure, LAU rocket launchers. The hand-held machine guns they had were also made in the United States. I could see that when they went right by where I was hiding.

"The bodies were burned to a crisp. You couldn't tell one person from another, except for a few guys who'd jumped out of the truck and had their throats slit by the contras and were lying alongside the truck. Those bodies didn't get burned."

Jorge Luís Briones ended his story: "I feel very, very angry with anybody who wants to murder people who haven't done any harm to anybody. My buddies had never been to war, they were civilians. All they wanted to do was do their work. The contras were sadists. That was their fun, what they did. And now I feel like grabbing a gun and getting rid of them, so they can't keep murdering innocent people, kids, like that little five-year-old boy that was along with us, and women. So they can't keep murdering the Nicaraguan people. Now more than ever, I feel like joining the national defense effort and putting a stop to this dirty war once and for all, this war that the U.S. president has forced us into."

REFUGEE BARRIO

On the outskirts of Estelí is a barrio or settlement of DPs, persons displaced by war, called "Barrio May 1982." Some 250 families live there, and whole *campesino* families, or remnants of families, continue to arrive. They have abandoned their villages, their homes, and their fields for fear of the contras, or Guards, as they call them indiscriminately—for fear of the Nicaraguan Democratic Force. This cooperative settlement was originally begun by victims of the 1982 floods, hence its name. But in that same year, 1982, *campesino* families terrorized by the kidnappings, pillaging, destruction, and arson they had suffered at the hands of the contras also began arriving. Since 1984, the new arrivals tend to be members of *campesino* cooperatives that have been destroyed and burned by the contras.

These settlements are living archives of the tragedies in which the contras are persecuting and impoverishing thousands of Nicaraguan *campesino* families. Anyone desiring first-hand contact with the sort of "liberation" the contras promote in Nicaragua with their dirty war might well begin here, with a visit to these victims.

Driven from Their Homes

I went to the main construction site of Barrio 1982 and con-- ducted six interviews, some brief, others more extended. I was told, for example, what the contras had done to *campesinos* of the Santo Domingo Cooperative, which had numbered eighty-six families. The Santo Domingo Cooperative was entirely undefended. After burning its installations and its stores of coffee, corn, and beans, the contras went in search of the workers. When they found them they shot them, cut their throats, tortured them, or ordered them to run so that they could use them as moving targets. "They burned Lucío Sánchez's tongue with their cigars. Then they shot him six times."

"We suffer much persecution," said one woman, a widow, who preferred that her name and that of her village not be used, for fear of reprisals by the contras. "My daughter was a literacy teacher. Some of my relatives had been murdered, others kidnapped. And we found out that the contras had a list and that we were on it— people to be killed. So we decided to come here. That was very hard for me. I felt badly. But now I have found some of my old friends here, in the Christian community."

Don Filemón Hernández: "We had a little coffee farm in Santo Domingo de Telpaneca. One night back in 1981, when I came in from the fields, I found a knife on the bed, with a note on it. The note said I'd better watch out, I was going to die. It was from the contras."

Angela Blandón, Palacio Blandón's widow: "My civilian cousins were threatened with death if they didn't go with the contras. They took Sebastián González Blandón. It's barbarity. It's an assault on the people."

Bernarda Rodríguez Gutiérrez de Lagos, widow of Santiago Lagos: "We lived just this side of Wiwilí. We worked in teams. We were attacked three times. They attacked Las Minas three times, too. Everything was ruined. There was nothing left."

Adilia Rugama de Valenzuela, wife of Julio César Valenzuela: "The poor have to be where there's work. It's the only way we can survive." And she told her "DP story." "We came here from Darailí, sixteen kilometers from Condega, in the department of Estelí, on the road to Yalí. There was a livestock and coffee ranch in Darailí. My husband was in charge of the livestock. On July 9, 1983, Comandante Tomás Borge arrived to distribute land titles to the *campesinos* of the cooperative. On July 12, we were informed that the contras were in the area and could easily come in and burn the whole thing down. So for a while we expected them. But by the twentieth the army had scoured the countryside and it no longer looked as if there were any contras around.

"On the twenty-first, my husband took all his workers out into the pastures. At eight o'clock in the morning they started hearing shots. But you heard a lot of that around there; we thought it was our army. Then a twelve-year-old girl that was spending her vacation with us said, 'Listen, Aunt Adi! That's not our army shooting!' Then the mortars started firing, first from one direction and then from the other, a tremendous hail of bullets started raining down, and those contras came screaming, 'Outa there, dogs, we're burning your whole thing down!' We were in a little hut a ways from the ranch house, and we could see how all the workers were running back up to the house, because nobody had any guns, they'd gone out to work, that's all, and they told everybody, 'Get back inside! It's the contras!' I grabbed all the kids and stuck them under the bed. They had a 'sixty' up on the other side of the house. Those mortar blasts were tremendous. Then we saw that the ranch house was on fire! I said, 'They're gonna kill us all this time, kids!' I figured they'd get my husband and kill him. They burned the ranch house to the ground, they burned the trucks, the tractors, and everything. The only things left were a store of coffee that didn't catch fire, and the kitchen, because they wanted to use the kitchen themselves after the operation.

"I'd drilled into my head what my husband had said to me—that if the contras ever came and he wasn't around I should head out a side way and get up to the road, about half-a-kilometer away. So I said to the kids, 'Let's go!' And away we went. As we left the little house, I could see how a couple of dozen contras were going off with all the *campesinos* there'd been in the ranch house. I had some money with me, the rent they'd paid me five days before for a little house I had in Estelí. Seven thousand pesos, in my knapsack. It was all we'd taken with us. But one of my kids saw some contras nearby and said, 'Ahhh! Mama! I'm scared!' And he grabbed for the sack. The sack broke and everything fell out. All the money was lost. We hid among some pines so the contras wouldn't find us. Then we came out and found a house, where they put us up for the night. I figured Dad had been killed or kidnapped. That's what I was thinking, that night, when a boy came up to the house and said, 'Doña Adilia, don't worry! Nothing happened to Don Julio!' He said he was in such-and-such a place, that he'd escaped. About five in the afternoon, the next day, he came to get us.

When we got back home there was nothing. They'd stolen everything, clothes and everything. We'd had a little milk cow. They'd stolen her too. They left us without anything. So about two months ago we came to Estelí.

"My husband told me how the contras had abducted sixty-seven *campesinos*. He said there were 365 contras. They're always counting themselves, that's how he knew. But when the Nicaraguan army started out after the contras, they scattered, and the *campesinos* from the ranch house got away. Only ten didn't get away, and they escaped a few days afterwards.

"Then the people rebuilt the ranch house, and they were working in teams, for safety. But last May the contras came back, and killed some *campesinos* and kidnapped some others. We don't know if they killed the others or if they're still in Honduras. Some bodies have been found, but others could still be alive in Honduras for all we know. And the contras burned San Jerónimo and Los Alpes, other co-ops. There's nothing left there. So if that's the way it was going to go, well, my husband didn't want to go back there. He found work here, in a shoemaking co-op. We poor have to be where there's work. It's the only way we can survive."

So Many Widows and Orphans

"My name is Audilia Herrera de Ochoa. I'm a widow. I'm fifty-three. I'm a practicing Christian, a member of the Assembly of God." Audilia is a forthright, expressive person. She wore a close-fitting suit and had her hair drawn back in a bun. Her voice was strong. "My daughter, Adaluz Ochoa, twenty years old, and my cousin, Ana Julia Ochoa, who taught school, were the two that the contras raped." And she gave me a long and detailed account, a tale of suffering.

"I lived in the village called Los Terreros, eighteen kilometers from Yalí. We had to have eyes in the back of our head. We could never work or sleep peacefully. One day the contras came, rousted us out, and said, 'Come out of there. You're all going to be shot. Get into the fields, because these houses are going to burn.' I was sick. I was lying in bed. But I got up. I heard a long, low moan. They'd hit a cow when they were machine-gunning a boy who was running away. I put myself in contact with the Lord, and I said

'Lord, be the one to speak—give me authority to speak to these people,' because what those people were doing was unmentionable. When I got up and appeared at the door, a lot of people were lined up out in the fields. The contras were going to machine-gun them. 'Come out of there, lady,' said the chief, 'get out of there, because the house is going to be burned.' But I said, 'Why are you going to burn my house? I don't know you, I don't even know who you are! I never did anything to you! I don't see how you can have anything against me when I don't even know you!' 'Come out of there,' he said. 'We're under orders, and my commander's orders are to get you out of there.' He was in radio contact with his troops. Then I said to him, 'Look, I'm not going to come out!' 'Out,' he said, and fired more rounds from his machine gun. But they had to leave me there as a hopeless case. And in the meantime everybody had run for it and there I was all by myself. And right on the spot, as they were going from house to house, they grabbed a poor guy who had on army boots—but he was retarded, I mean severely retarded—and they killed him right on the spot. They cut his throat. That was the first terrible thing I saw. Well, the whole valley was scared out of its wits. The contras were telling everybody to come out of their houses as they went from door to door. Now, I ask you, who's going to come out of their house in a situation like that? The terror, the horror, when those people have come through your village!

"In a week they came back and kidnapped my husband. Before this he'd hidden from them everywhere, but who'd have thought they'd be back in a week, with a task force that size? My husband had just asked me for lunch, and was turning on the news, when in comes a man, the leader, and some other guys carrying FALs. Without so much as a by-your-leave, the leader goes into the other room and starts going through papers. My girls held school back there—it was an adult education center. They burned our papers, books, notebooks, everything they could lay their hands on. We just stood there and shook in our boots, the girls and I. When the leader was done burning papers and doing all his hell-raising in there he said to my husband, 'What's your name?' My husband gave him his name. 'Well! It's been two weeks we've been looking for you, you bastard,' he said, and next thing you know he's set up a two-way radio on the patio and is contacting headquarters, to find out what to do. 'O Lord,' I said, 'grant us your help, my God, because we are to die here all innocent. May we not falter in this time of trial.' Because I felt like I was dead already.

"They had their guns trained on my husband. They were talking to him but he wasn't saying anything. 'What's the matter, can't you talk? You talk to the tin soldiers [the civil militia—Ed.] and help them, how about a few words for us, eh?' I went up to the leader and I said, 'You want to know what the matter is? I'll tell you what the matter is. You've scared him to death, that's why. Everybody's scared of you guys. Because what you fellows do isn't human, it's animal. It isn't even animal, because animals treat each other decently! What you do is lower than animals. Look how you've got him standing there!' And he said to me, 'And you, what do you all do here? What do you do for a living?' 'We work for a living,' I said. 'Look at the seed corn we've got there! We work for a living.' 'What are you afraid of, then?' he said. 'We're afraid because you kidnap boys, you kidnap old people, you kidnap little kids! And worst of all, what you guys do is you kidnap people because of what somebody tells you in the valley here. You're not fighting for a policy, you go around on personal vendettas between neighbors here in the valley! Somebody'll come to you and say, "You know, so-and-so bothers me." And you guys'll rub him out! You go on a "military expedition" and rub him out! You go around killing people for fun! You haven't got any policy you fight for at all!' And we argued and argued.

"Then they wanted to take my husband with them. But I told them, 'If you take him take me too. If he's going to pay for something he didn't do, we'll both pay. We're two in one flesh.'

"I got ready. I got the kids together, and I told them, 'Okay, kids, we're going with the soldiers.' But I couldn't make it. I was too sick. They took my husband and left the rest of us there.

"The next day my husband came home. 'Work,' they'd said. 'Don't meddle.' Then I said, fine, we've been cleared. We can breathe easy. But one night—it was May 5, 1984—at about midnight someone came knocking at the door. It was them. They had a list of names. They already had everybody else they wanted in the valley and now they wanted me and my daughter. I wouldn't budge. We fought, and they took my daughter. They raped her. Apparently the whole troop wanted to get her and then they'd kill her, because that's what they did to a cousin of mine, fourteen years old; a lot of guys raped her and then they killed her. But they didn't have time to finish when they had my daughter; they ran into a fight. The army came up on them and they had to fight. Then when the mortars started, a chief, it was Zacarías, gave the order, 'Every man for himself!' And my daughter got away. She was back in a week. She'd lived in a cave, for days, without eating. She was sick. I had them take her to Yalí. But incognito, because the contras would get down there once in a while.

"There's a co-op in the valley. There was a horrible massacre there. They killed eleven-year-old kids. I saw the atrocities. They murdered people and committed all sorts of abominations. And then they wear medals and crosses and carry a Bible! And they say they pray before committing their evils and Jesus tells them when they're going to win! 'That's Satan talking to you,' I told them. 'Your war hasn't got a future. Go to work, you men, don't be so lazy.'

"So when I see that those people have Reagan's support and financing, I don't know what the *Señor* Reagan is after. It must be to finish us all off, people who don't do anything to him, people who eat their bread with sweat on their faces, little people, people with no power, people only looking for beans and corn so they can live in peace, people trying to make something of themselves. I don't see how that man can be so lacking in conscience and not stop to think that there's a God that wants us to live too. He's never stopped to consider that. I pray that God may come into that man's heart, because the atrocities that that man's encouraging. . . . Doesn't he think he's ever going to die? Mr. Reagan has left so many widows and orphans in this land. Lord, does he believe in God and not see that?"

4

Campesino Cooperatives Destroyed

Some of the accounts I heard in Estelí described contra assaults on crop and livestock cooperatives. The destruction and dismemberment of the *campesino* cooperatives were two of the prime goals of the contras in their war in Nicaragua all through 1984. The contras make the cooperatives their targets, attack them, and destroy the goods, the organization, and the lives of the poor, the *campesinos*.

Under Somoza, there were no more than twenty private cooperatives in Nicaragua. However, between 1979—the year Somoza was overthrown—and 1985, Nicaragua created nearly a thousand production cooperatives and some two thousand credit unions and service cooperatives. This means that many thousands of *campesino* families—previously dispossessed, landless, and helpless, without organization—have now begun to have land and to live in their own community groups, helping one another and sharing with one another their aid and their housing, education, health, and production projects. The contras have totally or partially destroyed sixty of these *campesino* cooperatives in the departments of Jinotega, Matagalpa, Estelí, Nueva Segovia, Madriz, and Zelaya.

Contra attacks on cooperatives are operations of broad military scope. They are carried out by task forces of from one hundred to three hundred soldiers, with plenty of heavy weapons, mortars, machine guns, rockets, grenades, and rifles. These military operations against *campesino* civilian objectives have obliged the members of the cooperatives to arm themselves and organize into militias in order to defend both their livelihoods and the lives of their families. The *campesinos* would like to use their hands exclusively with the tools of their trade. They are laborers. But they see themselves obliged to work with a weapon in one hand to protect their fields, their harvests, their families, and their lives from the military assaults of the contras.

The contras have selected these poor *campesinos* as the target of their fire in order to do away with their cooperatives and their progress. If the contras can destroy the democracy that the *campesinos* are building in their cooperatives, they may hope that they will be able to force them to return to the past—a past of spoliation, disorganization, and dispersion.

In order to understand this, all one need do is visit the cooperatives that have been destroyed, and listen to the *campesinos* who have been subjected to the armed aggression of the contras and who have suffered the death of their family members and the forced dissolution of their cooperatives. It is enough to see their terror, their pain, as well as their indignation and their firm determination to go back to work and reorganize their cooperatives, redoubling their defenses.

I saw all of this, heard it, and verified it in my visit to the *campesinos* of Santiago Araúz Cooperative, in Lagartillo, in the Achuapa area. They had suffered a contra attack just a few days before my visit. It was an excellent opportunity to obtain authentic accounts of the shedding of the blood of the innocent civilians in these mountainous *campesino* regions. I had the feeling that this new cooperative, so recently attacked with mortar and rifle fire and arson, might well prove to be a clear symbol of this front in the contras' war.

I went to Achuapa from Somotillo, with a detour through El Sauce. Achuapa is in the department of León, the rest of which has not been affected by the contra war. But Achuapa is in the extreme north of the department, at the foot of the rugged mountains that stand between the departments of León and Estelí. El Lagartillo lies in these mountains themselves, and the contras did make an incursion there.

It was a long trip. I saw old silver mines, arid plains withered by the sun and the warm February wind, and—when we took the road up the mountain—the fertile valley of Achuapa. With me was Father Ángel Arnaiz, who, on the day we traveled, March 10, 1985, was on his way to Achuapa to bury the six *campesinos* of the cooperative who had been killed by the contras, five men and a young woman of twenty. The North American priest they called "Vincente" was along, too, "to take the truth back to the United States." He did not want to miss the opportunity to meet the El Lagartillo *campesinos* himself and hear their stories.

ACHUAPA: "THEY DESTROY WHAT WE BUILD"

In Achuapa I saw the pain and concern on the faces of the women and children who had been evacuated under fire from the contras and who were still refugees at the foot of their mountain. They were staying in the parish center and in several people's homes, and they were a picture of insecurity. "Only the men have gone back up," I was told. "They went back to the cooperative to work the land. We women and children were afraid to go with them. The Guard might come back any time. They've sent written threats against us, those of us from Lagartillo, because we stopped their attack, and they couldn't wreck everything the way they wanted to. They've threatened to come back and wipe us out."

Fermín Rivera García, twenty-six, who had come down to visit his wife and four children, told me this story: "Before we formed the co-op, everybody lived in separate little houses raising what little the land would grow. Sometimes we rented a small plot to sow corn on, or beans, to feed our kids. Sometimes we worked a landowner's farm. So we survived. But after the triumph of our revolution, those of us who had no land decided to organize in co-ops, because we saw that that was the only way we'd ever get out of our poverty and ignorance and some of the other problems that weigh us *campesinos* down. Our government started giving us land, and we registered our Santiago Aráuz Cooperative, up in Lagartillo, as early as 1982. We started to work. There are only twenty-seven families up there, but twenty-two work in the co-op. It's a farm co-op—corn, beans, and livestock, for example. The school, too, was built by the community. And besides the co-op families themselves, relatives and neighbors would send their kids to school there, and then the kids would help in the co-ops. And later we had a housing project. It was already under construction. We'd already built one house.

"We were very hopeful about our co-op work. It looked as if it would provide for everybody. Sure, we knew the contras were our enemies. They're the old Guard. We knew they could come in any minute and slaughter us. Before the revolution, any time the people would try to do anything worthwhile, the Guard would come and wreck it, and the contras keep doing the same thing. The Somozist tyranny never let the *campesinos* get ahead. So we knew we could be attacked by the contras. They destroy what we build. And they kill people, including children and teenagers, anybody at all.

"The day it happened, about eight in the morning, two of the men had gone down to Achuapa. The rest stayed up in the co-op. There were twelve or thirteen of us men up there, then, including a young twenty-year-old and two boys of about fifteen. We had no army people with us. We were all civilians. We did have weapons, but it was only in case they came to slaughter us. I was hoeing young corn, about eight in the morning. A buddy was putting up a fence nearby. The others were doing something else, and, as I say, two of the men were on the way to Achuapa. About nine, a gentleman came over from San Nicolás to tell us the contras were heading for the co-op. He said they'd clubbed him just because he always worked for the good of the region, because he planted whatever the community needed. He was a nice guy to come over and warn us. He prevented a lot of slaughter in the co-op. There were over fifty kids and about thirteen women with us. So, after I'd been hoeing the corn for an hour or two, this gentleman drags himself over there somehow and warns us that the contras are coming. We get all the women and children together in one place. And all the rest of us, the few that we had, get ready to see what we could do about defending ourselves, because it was going to be slaughter now—we knew that this was what the Guards loved to do, slaughter co-op people. They don't like us to organize, they don't like progress, they don't like you to have a school, they don't like family welfare—let alone co-ops.

"The Guard came in from the south and made a semicircle around us. Nobody was our leader; we all just took positions and got ready to defend ourselves. I stayed with the families, and the bullets were flying, but I managed to get some of the women and kids out. We took them to where we didn't think the Guards would be shooting, a drainage ditch up on the hill. I got my whole family up there. The other guys started fighting the Guards. We were outnumbered, of course, with thirteen of us against 250 Guards.

"The attack lasted about two hours. They fired at us with mortars and all kinds of weaponry. The plan they had was to surprise us and kidnap the whole co-op, children, women, and men. They figured they'd kill anybody who tried to stop them, kidnap the rest, and burn and destroy everything. But we'd been warned by that gentleman, and we defended ourselves.

"So they were only able to burn the school. They totally destroyed the school, and burned all the furniture. They burned all the belongings of two families that lived in the school, along with a little store of grain we had in there. And they killed six of our people—five men and a girl, Zunilda Pérez. They killed her dad, too. But we resisted and they ran for it. They couldn't take the houses because we were defending them. So they ran back the way they came.

"After they were gone we gathered up the bodies and brought them here to Achuapa. We buried them. We'd always leave two or three people up there guarding the co-op, though. We never abandoned the co-op. We didn't want anybody just coming in and grabbing what they could find. Since then we've stayed up there and kept working the co-op, and the women take turns feeding us, two or three of them at a time, usually about noon. The women are really scared. They're afraid the Guards will come back. But we did it before and we can do it agian. We've got to keep at it. Right is on our side, and we're not going to quit. We're ready to hang on to the bitter end. We're not going to abandon our co-op, not for a moment."

Florentina Pérez, the woman who lost her husband, Ángel, and her twenty-year-old daughter, Zunilda, is thirty-six. She has four children left. She is thin and spirited. She was in work pants and a blue-checked blouse, very clean and freshly ironed. Her face is dark and placid. She wore her hair in one long, thick braid in back. It was an effort for her to control her emotion as she spoke.

"I had the feeling none of us was going to get out of this

alive, because when we were told, 'The contras are coming!' they were practically at the school already. Our first thought was to head for a shelter, but the shelter was so small and there were so many of us women and kids, so we thought it'd be better to run for it. And we ran for it. I went on ahead, with three of my children. The oldest one, Zunilda, the moment they said, 'The contras are coming!' grabbed an AKA, and there she was, on her way, with an AKA in one hand and a sack of ammunition in the other. The only thing I said to her was, 'Little girl, are you going to wear that white blouse?' And I ran and got her a brown one. She put it on and left again. When I came out on the patio again I saw her running over right where I figured the contras'd be coming from. So I called to her not to go over that way. She came back, and then I couldn't see which way she went.

"So there I was, with the three little ones, running, and I met my husband. So I asked him, 'Where shall we head?' 'Follow Valentín,' he told me, 'he'll take you.' But I saw that Velantín was looking for a place over by where I figured the contras were coming from. So I didn't follow him, I ran the other way. But I hadn't run any distance at all when the first shots rang out. So I dived into a ditch with the three kids. Then I saw the very first one getting ready to fire his mortar. And I thought, 'They're coming in and they're going to finish us off if we stay here.' And I said, 'Run, kids!' But as soon as we started running they started shooting at us. We could hear the bullets whizzing around our heads. You could hear them landing in the brush, all those bullets! I just looked around to see how many kids they'd gotten. But thank God, the kids were still running. And we managed to get back behind a mound. They couldn't hit us there. I got a bullet through my blouse, back here, while I was running. After that the only thing I could think of was, why were there just ten of them that'd stayed behind, why did two of them have to head on down the mountain today, of all days, and I never thought we'd survive, because I could hear bombs going off, mortars, everything they had they threw at us. And I could tell there were lots of contras and only ten of us. All along the way all I did was cry, figuring they were all dead.

"We climbed up some big, rough gullies, till we got to the top, with all the kids. There were sixty kids, from two to ten. There were ten of us women with them. We got to what they call the Abajo

River, and from there down here, to Achuapa village.

"About five in the afternoon we got word who'd been killed. I was desperate to hear, but I thought I might as well go back and look for myself, because I figured they were all dead. A boy came down about five o'clock and I ran to ask him who was dead. He just told me, 'José Ángel and Zunilda.' He didn't say who the others were. When they got the bodies here I could see for myself."

Florentina told me all of this in great calm. Her black eyes filled with tears, but she did not weep audibly.

I asked her what she intended to do now with her life and her children. She answered very firmly: "I'm going to stay. When they tell me, 'All right, you can come back to the co-op now,' I'm going back. I'll never give them the pleasure of getting what they're after. What they're after is to wreck the co-ops. I'll never give them that satisfaction. I'll die first. When they tell me, 'You can come on back now,' I'm going to go back to the co-op with my kids. I'll never give in to what they're after. And I've said already that now I *am* going to work on learning to be a good shot, because I don't know how to shoot. They're not going to make a fool out of me the next time I see them coming. It's like my little girl had said. She said, 'Mom, if the contras ever come here, I'm not going to run away, and I'm not going to let them take me alive, because all you have to do is see the atrocities they do—I'd rather die than run away or surrender!' That's what she told me. And that's what she did. I didn't think she had such courage. But she did."

Florentina was momentarily unable to go on. Finally she began again. "I plan to stay, and go back up to the co-op. In spite of the threats. A few days after they came in with that savage attack, they went to Guanacaste, and left a note on the door of the school. It said, 'Lagartillo: Don't try to stop us again, or it'll be worse than the last time.' That's what they wrote. I'm going to stay because their war is wrong and our co-op is right. They fight for what is not theirs. The contras are just the same Guards as under Somoza, and now they fight because the United States is helping them and showing them how to do it. The one whose fault it is is the president of the United States, since he's the one supplying them with everything. They're just like puppy dogs, you whistle and they come."

I watched Florentina pick up her youngest child, Cony (Concepción), three years old. The little girl told me, very clearly, "The contras came and killed Zunildita and my daddy and Javier."

Florentina handed Cony to the child's grandmother for a moment, mounted her horse, took the child back from the grandmother, and rode off. The grandmother, Baltasara Pérez, mother of José Ángel Pérez, then told me, "They weren't ready for a fight. They were working and the contras just came and killed them."

The last interview I had in Achuapa was with the wife of Fermín Rivera—Rufina Pérez de Rivera, twenty-six, mother of four—and with Genara Pérez de Gutiérrez, twenty-three, mother of two children and six months pregnant. (Here it's the Pérezes, I thought to myself. Over there it was the Espinozas, the Quinteros, the Ponces—big families, workers, united, hothouses of *campesino* leadership.) Rufina and Genara told me: "It was horrendous. We ran away with the kids right through the fighting. Some we let run by themselves, some we carried, and we all headed for the big gullies up there, scared they'd kill us because maybe they'd see us and shoot at us. The kids were scared out of their wits. They were terrified. A lot of them were crying. Some were quiet, but the little ones cried. They're still scared, the kids are.

"It's hard now. It's not easy with all these kids running around. It's not so easy to live in the village here and watch the days go by. In the co-op we were together, we all worked, there was love, we were friends. It's hard to be the way we are now. But we have hope, and we're determined. We're going back, because if we don't we'll give them the satisfaction! They'll laugh at us if we don't go back. And they've killed all those men! We can't leave the co-op after a sacrifice like that. We'll keep on with the co-op. It's our life."

I observed that for the *campesinos* of Achuapa as well for the others I had spoken with—and they have a sharp eye for what's what and who's who—"the contras are just the same Guards as under Somoza." And I observed that the cooperatives are indeed the *campesinos'* liberation and their life. This is why they would rather die than abandon them.

Their accounts left a clear outline of the principal objective of the military actions of the contras in the war they are waging: the destruction of the cooperatives in which the poor *campesinos* have begun to organize. My observation was to be confirmed by the impressive testimony of two North American church people whom I would interview in Managua. To this interview I devote the final chapter of this chronicle of innocent blood in Nicaragua.

5

Testimony of a North American Priest and Nun

A goodly number of missionaries from the United States—
priests and nuns alike—are in Nicaragua. They work in all regions,
including the war zones. After I had conducted and recorded the
above interviews with Nicaraguans, once back in Managua I
thought it important to hear from some missionaries from the
United States about their personal experience of Nicaragua and
about what their judgment might be of the sufferings they had seen
among the civilian population in the zones in which the contras
operate.

I selected a priest and a nun from the United States. The priest,
James Feltz, is pastor of Bocana de Paiwas, in the extreme south-
east of the department of Matagalpa, a lovely region of mountains
and forests—the forests of Zelaya. The nun, Sandra Price, of the
Congregation of Notre Dame de Namur, works with the pastoral
team of the parish of Siuna, in the Vicariate Apostolic of
Bluefields, department of Zelaya Norte.

After listening to these missioners from the United States, I had
occasion to observe that their opinions and judgment in no way
diverged from the consensus of the other North American priests
and religious in Nicaragua. There are always missionaries from the
United States participating in the weekly demonstrations and protests held in front of the U.S. Embassy in Managua, demonstrations and protests against U.S. State Department policy in its
support and aid to the contras.

From the way James Feltz and Sandra Price spoke with me, I could tell they had given a great deal of thought to their views and judgments, which they based on their own direct experience. The interview with these two was quick and simple. I had only to ask them to relate to me their personal experience with the civilians, mostly poor *campesinos*, and to tell me how, in light of what they had seen in the regions where they worked, they judged President Reagan's policy of legitimation of, support for, and aid to the contras. After that all I had to do was listen.

JAMES FELTZ

"It's Like Death Swooping Down"

James Feltz, forty-seven, a native of Milwaukee, was ordained to the priesthood in 1970.

"I'm a priest from the United States who has been in Nicaragua for three-and-a-half years. Previously I spent seven years as a missionary in Peru, and before that, three years of priestly work with Mexicans in Chicago. I came to Nicaragua in 1981 by invitation of Bishop Salvador Schlaefer, of Zelaya. I'm incardinated in his Vicariate of Bluefields, and he's my ecclesiastical superior, as he is Vicar Apostolic of Bluefields.

"I'd no sooner arrived in Paiwas and taken over as pastor when one of the communities, Santa Rosa, suffered an attack by the contras. This was in August 1981. Two or three *campesinos* died. I didn't know them. They were just names to me. But it was my first contact with contra violence.

"The first painfully personal experience I had was on March 3, 1982, in Copalar, another community of the parish. We were holding a mission there. We were meeting with the Catholic Action Committee when seven armed men walked in, pointed their guns at us, and intimidated the whole group of Christians there. They told us that if we had anything to do with the revolutionary process it'd go hard with us indeed. And after harassing, threatening, and intimidating everybody, they bragged that they had just killed the town judge. One of them had a great deal of blood on his shirt. The murdered judge's name was Emiliano Pérez Obando, and was a

Delegate of the Word of God in the parish of Paiwas. They said they'd left him to die not far away, but that anyone who went to help him was under 'sentence of death.' So we two priests had to go looking for Emiliano, because even after the contras had left, to go looking for the house of a certain *campesino* they wanted, nobody in the room dared move for fear of being under that 'death sentence.' Nobody dared move a muscle.

"We found Emiliano wounded and dying. His body was still warm, but he was near death. We had hopes that if we could get him to a doctor or a hospital we might be able to save his life. We borrowed a car and raced away. Emiliano was lying on my lap. I tried to console him, communicate with him, unconscious though he was.

"On the way to Río Blanco, Emiliano died in my arms. He had ten kids and another on the way. It was terribly hard for me to have to go and tell his widow that this so courageous person was dead. He had done his duty as judge in spite of the danger of death to anyone in a position of responsibility in the area. He was a just judge, determined to do his duty without double-talk or pussyfooting. And he was exemplary as Delegate of the Word in the parish for years. His murder was a very heavy blow for the whole population of the parish, the town, and all of the villages of the region. He'd been a real Christian and a good judge who'd served everybody with real enthusiasm and generosity. He was admired by many people. This was my first close contact with the contras in all their savage brutality. I could see the contras didn't have a trace of humanity left. I saw how they boasted of having murdered this person, and how they enjoyed intimidating people. I saw how they'd enjoyed murdering Emiliano.

"Another of the several cases I've experienced firsthand was an attack by a contra task force toward the end of August and early September 1983. A task force of five hundred contras had worked its way into our territory, under a certain Renato, an ex-Somozist Guard who had previously worked in the Río Blanco zone. He and his group came first to the little village of Anito, a little cluster of about eight houses on the bank of the Río Grande de Matagalpa. They had no defense there, maybe one poor militia guy with a BZ. The contras came in with mortars. They mortared the chapel. They blew off part of the roof and wrecked some of the wooden walls on the inside. But this was only their spearhead. This was only sixty contras. They came in and dragged everybody out into the road, after killing a *campesino* on the way in. Then they killed another, who happened to be drunk, in cold blood. The drunk thought they were Sandinistas and began praising the Sandinistas, in his drunken way, and they shot him on the spot. He'd never belonged to any organization. They just shot him to keep from having to listen to him, even though he was obviously drunk.

"So they got everybody out onto the road, didn't let them take anything with them, and set fire to their houses. Then they kept going, deeper into the area. They ran into various *campesinos*. They tore a Bible out of the hands of one Delegate of the Word. They did that to impress the *campesinos* in the zone by going around showing them the Bible themselves, when they would say what great Christians they were and how they were doing all this for Jesus Christ. They would try to win over the young people and get them to join their side. And to attract them, they'd tell them they had Reagan's support. And they'd flash money, big bills. They'd make a point of explaining that they get lots of money from Reagan and could buy anything they wanted. They killed six people in that area. Then they crossed the river and continued their march. It's like death swooping down, it's like Attila's hordes.

"From the other side of the river, the contras could see the group of houses where they'd killed two *campesinos*, and they could see the people gathering to bury them. There they were, the people, around the graves, at prayer—and from the other side of the river, the contras mortared them. Then they went on to another area, and killed three more people, very brutally. One was hanged from the roof of his house. The others had their throats cut, and one his eyes gouged out.

"On they went, to the little hamlet or cluster of houses called Las Minitas, where they hauled the people out of their houses again. One house there belonged to a woman named Mila González, who worked in the parish. We have a picture of her renewing her baptismal promises during her investiture as a member of the pastoral team. She and her husband bore the expenses of the ministry in the community. They hauled her out, questioned her, and then let her go. But when they'd left, a guy in the region with a chip on his shoulder denounced her. They came back, dragged her about five hundred meters from the hamlet, and 'executed' her, shamelessly—made her get down on her knees and shot her in cold blood, put a bullet through her brain.

"They burned a number of homes in that same area. Then they headed for the region around El Guayabo. On the way they ran into a man named Sotelo—'Chico' Sotelo. Chico had livestock and was not much for the revolution. Certainly he was no Sandinista. He had his money and his private property. But he made the mistake of pulling out his UNAG passbook. Well, all they had to do was see he belonged to the Unión Nacional de Agricultores y Ganaderos, the farmers' union, and they shot him on the spot, right out there on the road. He didn't even live in the neighborhood. He was passing through. And just because he carried this passbook, which is nothing extraordinary at all, they killed him. And they kept burning houses. The death march got as far as El Guayabo. There there's a little hamlet called San Francisco, and they killed several people there; they killed people if they were members of defense committees or shopkeepers or maybe members of the militia. But nobody was armed. They raped a fourteen-year-old girl. Then they slit her throat and cut off her head. They hung the head on a pole along the road. This was the second time they had murdered someone and cut off the head and hung it up to frighten and intimidate the people.

"In this same hamlet they dragged three women, relatives of other victims, out into the road, made them line up for execution, and ordered them to get down on all fours. Scared to death, the women got down on the ground like pigs. And the contras fired on them with a machine gun. One was killed, another wounded. The third was unhurt.

"There was another special case of cruelty on that same contra operation. An eleven-year-old girl, Cristina Borge Díaz, was visiting her uncle. The uncle was on the contras' list, and they came and killed him. When they saw the little girl, they decided to have a little fun. So they used her for target practice. The first one took a shot at her from a galloping horse. He missed. 'Kill her,' he told a companion. And the other shot her in the back. The bullet came out her chest. Another bullet grazed her scalp, another hit her in the right hand, and another in the left hip. Then they left. The little girl lay there until a worker coming back from the fields found her that way, more dead than alive. He took her to her home and helped attend to her. Her mother had had too much to drink that day, and once she understood what had happened, she became so frightened she was unable to act. She was afraid to take the girl out of the house because she thought the contras would catch them and kill them. The father had malaria and was delirious. Because of the raids, the area was in some chaos—people in remote areas were cut off from one another, and somehow the people in the area didn't understand the severity of what had happened to the girl. Nobody came by. So the little girl stayed in the house for over a week till I arrived on September 19. Here's a picture of her at her house with her wounds. We got her out of there, took her to Managua, had some operations and a skin-graft on the leg, and the little girl's all right! She recovered. She was recovering all by herself when I got to her house. A real miracle.

"This is a case that seems to me to present a real problem. How could they use a little girl for target practice? The cruelty of the contras is unbelievable. They killed twenty people, this task force of Renato's, on this one barbaric operation."

(A few days after this interview, Father Feltz took Cristina to Managua, to a meeting of missionaries from the United States with the delegation of U.S. Bishops that visited Nicaragua from February 24 to 27, 1985. Cristina showed the bishops, priests, and sisters her scars and told her story.)

"There were kidnappings, too, of course, on that same operation. The contras abducted twenty-five *campesinos* in all. I remember one of them very well, because I spoke with him afterwards—after he'd managed to escape and get back. He told me what he had had to go through. His name is Francisco Pérez. He's a simple, poor man, who interferes with nobody—a calm, quiet guy. He was sixty years old, and they made him carry a drum of some liquid they had along. They ate only once a day, and very little even then. The prisoners were not allowed to stop to rest, even though they were carrying loads like that, and they kept going for five days. Then there was fighting, and he was able to get away in the confusion. He was a long way from home, though, and by the time he arrived home his feet were all torn up. An hour later he couldn't walk. He'd hidden in various ranch houses on the way back, for fear he'd meet up with the contras again. He told me that the contras showed the abductees no mercy, and that they lived in constant fear of being 'executed.' This is what happened to one of the twenty-five that were taken on that day.

"After this incursion, and such a beastly one, the whole population of the area was terror-stricken. And so they decided to group in hamlets for their own protection. They formed little militia squads in the area and organized co-ops, to raise a few pigs. There were twelve families in each co-op, sharing production, defense, education, and a health program. The project moved ahead because the people of the region supported it.

"There were to be twenty-four cooperatives in the project. Nine had already begun when in May 1984 there was another incursion in the area, by a big task force this time, some eight hundred contras. I personally saw them entering the area because I was out on mission and ran into them. They intimidated me, too, insisting that a minister of God surely couldn't support the revolutionary process when the Sandinistas in charge of the revolution were 'not of God' and didn't even believe in God. They told me that God was on their side, the contras' side. They figured that anybody doing pastoral work with the poor of my parish, who were in such great need and so terrorized by the crimes of the contras, must be actively supporting the Sandinistas. You wonder what they imagine God thinks of the sort of thing they go around doing. Well, on May 8, when this task force entered the northern quarter of the parish, as I saw them cross to the south I realized that they might be going to attack those little clusters of homes and cooperatives that were beginning to form their little territorial militia squads in the southern quarter of the parish. It was extremely frustrating not to be able to warn the region, but the contras had me under observation. And on May 13, at dawn, the contras attacked the militia of El Jorgito.

"The results were tragic. The people of El Jorgito were just completing construction of a little command post for their new militia. The *campesino* militia had decided to celebrate the opening with their families. It was insanity, given the circumstances, with the contras so nearby. But the militia had not been advised of the proximity of the contras. There was no communication, they had no radios, and so they had no idea that a contra task force was so near with their heavy weapons. And they celebrated the opening. This meant a festival. This meant dancing, this meant drinking, this meant drunkenness. The whole area had gathered together for a family festival, with a record player and everything. They danced till dawn.

"At four-thirty or five the contras attacked. And they attacked without any consideration for whether they were shooting militia or civilians or women or children. They could have come in with ten men under arms and taken the command post without spilling a drop of blood, without destruction, without murdering civilians. But the contras don't do things that way. They surrounded the post with three hundred troops and fired mortars, grenades, and rifles. They launched a surprise mortar attack with all of the people inside. They took the first line of defense, the outer trenches, and from there they lobbed thirty hand grenades on the people. In two hours they killed thirty-five *campesinos* of the area, including five women and nine children. The owner of the record player, who was from another district and who had come only to be of service by providing his record player for the occasion, was killed, along with his son, whom he'd brought along. Neither had any connection with the militia or with anything else. A number of co-op members were killed. The whole Juárez family died. Matos Juárez was a Delegate of the Word of God and chairperson of the Catholic Action Committee in El Jorgito. He was responsible for the chapel and functioned as minister of baptism in this district. He died at dawn on May 13.

"That was the height of contra murder and terror in that region. Since then the people have taken refuge in Paiwas. They're separated from their land and separated from their homes. They've lost their animals and their clothing. They have no lands and see no future for themselves. They're refugees. Now, though, there's the possibility they might be resettled on other farms, on the outskirts of Paiwas. Their fear of the contras is total. Many no longer are even willing to enlist as catechists or Delegates of the Word, for fear of getting on the wrong side of the contras. They know that the contras persecute all this sort of thing. Of course, the contras call themselves Christians.

Father Feltz went on: "When I see all this suffering, and all this barbarity on the part of the contras against the *campesino* people, and I know perfectly well that the U. S. government under Reagan is giving such extensive and direct aid and support to the contras,

I'm very ashamed. . . . It's so clear that the contras don't have any positive program to offer. They don't have any plan for the development of the country. You can see from what they're doing right now that they wouldn't support a literacy program among the people, they wouldn't support the formation of health brigades, they wouldn't support any of the services that the people now have. Land reform? Forget it. The contras have spoken out explicitly against agrarian reform by destroying the *campesino* co-ops. What a monstrous contradiction that the United States, in the name of democracy, is lending support to a potential regime that would be and already is so destructive and cruel toward the *campesinos*. It's a great, great contradiction. . . .

"Aid to the contras is immoral. No justification that is being advanced will hold water. To call the contras 'freedom fighters' and to compare them with the historic liberators, with Simón Bolívar, with the framers of the United States constitution, with the resistance to the Nazi occupations, is a travesty. It's either cynicism or shameful ignorance."

SANDRA PRICE

"The Contras Are Killing the Poorest and Most Innocent People"

Sandra Price is from California. She is forty-two, and a religious of the Congregation of Notre Dame de Namur.

"I celebrate my silver jubilee as a religious this year. I've been in Nicaragua since 1981. Since February 1982 I've been working in Costa Atlántica—I'm with another sister (a *campesina* and native of the region) in the township of Siuna, a village of miners and *campesinos* nearly 150 kilometers from Puerto Cabezas, department of Zelaya Norte. I do pastoral and social work, not in the village itself, but in the *campesino* communities that belong to the parish—some forty-eight communities. The *campesinos* make their living growing basic cereal commodities. This is their livelihood. Most of the men and children learned to read and write in the National Literacy Crusade, but I don't think the majority of the adult women are literate. A pastoral team of three—the pastor, the other sister, and myself—work for the advancement of women, especially in a context of the farming cooperatives. And we work with the Delegates of the Word of God in the training of pastoral ministers. We receive financial support from the bishop for our work, since this is part of the pastoral work of the parish of Siuna, which belongs to the Vicariate Apostolic of Bluefields. Our bishop is Bishop Salvador Schlaefer. We are his co-workers.

"I was sent to this mission by my religious superiors. My congregation's general chapter takes responsibility for my work, supports it, and approves of it. Just in these last days the superiors of the general chapter have been here and have seen the work we do. In every country in which we have communities, my religious congregation has groups in solidarity with us called 'Project Nicaragua.'

"Since we've come to this area we've seen a tremendous increase in acts of violence on the part of the contras against the civilian population. Contra terrorism is constantly on the increase. The victims are the people. We see that most of the attacks are directed against defenseless persons, innocent of any involvement in military affairs. We've seen how the country has had to increase its military presence in our region, owing to the stepped-up contra attacks on the defenseless *campesinos*.

"In recent months we've had terrible attacks on the people. This gives us a new awareness, and tremendous pain. There have been cruel attacks on the co-ops and on the people who live in the region where the contras pass through and commit every sort of abuse, persecution, kidnapping, and murder. We might as well say that the *campesinos* are prisoners in the mountains, prisoners of the contras. The *campesinos* don't dare try to go to the village, and so they're deprived of everything they don't produce themselves. They can't have clothes, sugar, soap, or so many other necessary things. The contras won't let them move—they think they're on the way to give information to the Sandinistas. And they threaten them and lie to them, telling them that if the Sandinistas come to the village they're going to take them prisoner. So the people are frightened to death to move. Many communities have simply disappeared, owing to the contras kidnappings and terrorism.

"Every day we hear of more kidnappings. Last week they ambushed a public transport bus, killed the soldier who was accompanying it, and robbed the passengers. They were going to abduct them too, but thank God a truckload of militia came along, about ten men, and fired into the air—so they wouldn't hit any civilians—

and the contras fled. Even the main road is becoming dangerous. When we go out on the road we don't know whether our lives are safe or not—contra ambushes are constant and completely reckless of the safety and lives of the people.

"We've visited families that have suffered tremendously. There's a family in the parish that's very close to us—the dad's a Delegate of the Word of God. They've had to move five times. They're on the contras' list. Their story began in the old days of the Somozist Guard. A number of relatives had been killed by the Gaurd, and now the contras are after them. The contras today are simply keeping up the old, bloody persecution of this family carried out by the Guard, simply because after the triumph of the revolution this Delegate of the Word and his family helped people in two hamlets to organize. So threats from the contras began to arrive. The contras were going to kill them. Two years after the triumph they had to move. They went elsewhere and tried to organize a co-op—which isn't military and doesn't have anything to do with the military. Organizing a co-op is a simple right of the *campesino* people, and it is legitimate and right, a matter of justice and a basic right in any democracy—but the contras came, killed the president of the cooperative, and the whole cooperative was dispersed. So they moved again. The contras came again, kidnapped the eldest boy and some others, and the community had to be evacuated. So they moved again, formed another cooperative closer to the village, and the contras launched a horrible attack on the cooperative this past November 5, 1984. It was the Ulí Cooperative. So I ask, who's against democracy in Nicaragua? I think it's the contras.

"I want to tell you what I saw and heard in that co-op after the contras attacked it. I got there about five hours after the attack, at night. I was tremendously impressed when I saw that some twenty-four people—poor, simple *campesinos*—had defended their co-op for five hours against some three hundred contras with all their mortars, machine guns, and riflery. The women and children had gone to the shelters.

"I saw people reeling under a terrible blow, and in the depths of despair. Six members of the co-op had been killed—people who had done no more than unite in common life and common toil, in organized fashion, so that they wouldn't have to keep on living in isolation in the mountains. By living and working together they thought they could help one another more and make better progress. This was their 'crime.' This was the only crime they'd committed. Nobody in the army was there. There was no military post. These people had absolutely nothing to do with the military whatsoever. There were only civilians there, *campesino* laborers—women who didn't know how to read, men barely literate, Delegates of the Word, Christians, practicing Catholics every last one. These people hadn't done a thing. It was a horrible experience to see children who'd been burned when mortar fire struck at the entrance of the shelters. Two of the dead were a little old man and a deaf-mute child, who'd left the shelter before the attack was over. I was terribly moved by the pain of these innocent people. The bodies had been left lying there, the six corpses. When I arrived, there they were, all twisted, lying just as they'd fallen. Two brothers had died together—they'd been in the same ditch and a mortar had hit right there and killed them both. Both of their two brothers had been wounded. The contras nearly wiped out that family. A tremendous anguish came over me, seeing the injustice of this absurd, cruel attack. And I felt something I'd never felt in my life—I felt strongly that if I had been there at the moment of the attack I'd have been capable of taking up arms to defend those innocent people, all of those *campesino* children and women and men.

"The other sister, who's a *campesina* herself and a native of that locality, is raising a little boy who was brought to us as a survivor of a massacre of a family by the contras on November 20, 1984. This happened in Coperna. The contras came to the house and killed the dad and mom, killed the little boy's young uncle, the uncle's bride, and a four-year-old boy. The little boy we have was orphaned at the age of six days. I have the story from a twelve-year-old girl who survived along with the little boy and another little brother of hers, eight years old. The contras came one night and machine-gunned the house. There were six children in the house with their parents, sleeping. One bullet killed a little boy in bed. Another bullet hit the legs of the dad, and also of the other little boy, the eight-year-old. Another bullet wounded the mom in the head. Then the contras came into the house and dragged the dad and the uncle outside. They asked them for their 'weapons.' There were no weapons in the house. Then they shot them—four shots. The first killed the young uncle. The dad was wounded again, then they cut his throat. Then they came back into the house. The bride was already dead. One contra looked at her and said, 'This bitch is Mariano's sister—you know, the tin soldier.' Her brother is in the militia. And they fired more shots into her dead body.

"The mom was still alive. The little girl told me that after it was all over the children said to her, 'Mommy, let's get away!' and that the mother had replied, 'Yes, kids, go, all go!' And the kids took the six-day-old baby and the other little boy, who'd been seriously wounded, and walked for an hour or more to the nearest house, where another uncle lived. They spent the night there. The next morning they returned to their own house. By now the mother was dead. They ran back to the uncle's house, and then returned to their own with an adult. Now they found nothing. The bodies were gone. Three days later, relatives found the bodies in the river. The contras had stripped the mother and the uncle's young bride naked. All the skin had been torn off the mom's face.

"The boy's leg was so badly wounded that he's still in the hospital. The other three children are with an aunt, who is also raising other orphans. They're all in a farming co-op. The aunt wasn't able to take the new baby with so many other children. Nor could the hospital take him. So Sister is raising him.

"There occurrences have produced tremendous rage and anguish in us. What cruelty and injustice! We see the contras hurting and killing the poorest and most innocent people in Nicaragua. And it's still greater cruelty, it's even more criminal, to aid and abet the contras and call them 'freedom fighters' and 'fighters for democracy' as President Ronald Reagan does. There's no word for that sort of criminal behavior. And I say this as a person from the United States who is on the spot and who sees the facts with my own eyes."

"I've Met the Contras Three Times"

"I've met the contras three times. The first time it was an ambush. We were driving along in a pick-up. We were all civilians. The contras stopped us along the road because they needed a battery. I thought they were going to kidnap us because they made us all get out, took us up a ridge, and gave us a political lecture, beginning with their interpretation of religion. They always begin the same way. You can tell they're reciting something they've been taught to say. Their religion lectures are intended to convince people that they're Christians and that the Sandinistas persecute the church and suppress religion. Of course nobody can really believe them in view of the facts. They can't believe it themselves! They know they're lying.

"This time the contras didn't know I was a nun. To them I was just one more in the group. They asked us what religion we belonged to, and then began to try to convince us that the Sandinistas persecute the church. They'd talk about facts and events, but they had them completely twisted around. I knew the facts and I could see that they didn't. I could see them changing things, inventing things, adding things, and generally mixing things up.

"As they were giving us this line, a truckload of Sandinista army regulars came along the road. The contras opened fire. Luckily, the Sandinistas didn't return the fire. They might have killed civilians. Then the contras left. They simply left us there and went off to attack a co-op. We heard the shooting as we were walking.

"My other two encounters with the contras were very similar. We were on a mission, in various areas, the parish priest, the other sister, and I. On the way we ran into the contras coming along with a big group of civilians. I don't know if they were abducting them but they said they were going to arm them. They kept us in the chapel all the rest of the day and all night. They threatened the priest, plenty. They accused him of involvement in politics and of being a communist. They told him that if he kept it up they were going to kill him. The next day another group of contras found a flyer in the chapel on the amnesty law, and even though they didn't have any evidence of who'd put it there, for them it was politics and the guilty party was the priest. So they threatened him even more. We thought they were going to abduct him. But it didn't turn out that way, and we finished our mission tour without further mishap.

"The priest continued to receive death threats. Another time, on our way to another chapel, we received word that the contras were waiting to abduct him, and we turned around and went back. Finally, on Radio September 15, the contras' station, we heard them call for the priest's murder. The international community should be provided with this priest's name right now. It's Enrique Blandón. He's under death threat from the contras. Now if anything happens to him everyone will know who's responsible.

"After so many death threats we decided that the priest

shouldn't go on mission tours any more. I went by myself the next time, with a few *campesinos* up to a certain point, and then continued to the chapel alone. There I invited anyone who wished to come along. A couple and a young woman catechist accepted. When we arrived at the other chapel a group of contras was waiting. They questioned me. They wanted to know if I 'preached politics.' But politics for them is anything having to do with people's actual life. For example, the contras killed the daughter of a Delegate of the Word simply because before the elections he had read the community a list of the political parties in Nicaragua. He thought they should be informed. For the contras this is politics, and so they killed his daughter and persecuted him. He had to leave his farm and his livestock. Well, they interrogated me there in the chapel, and I learned they were waiting for the priest—whether to kill him or kidnap him I don't know, anything's possible. I told them that the priest wasn't coming. They told me I was lying. Then they explained what nice people they were, and how we had nothing to fear from them, for they did no evil, and then they left. But the next day other contras came and kidnapped the couple. I tried to stop them—I said, 'So you weren't telling the truth last night!' There was tension for a moment, but they went off with the couple. This was so hard for me. Later they took the girl too, the catechist.

"I kept making the rounds as best I could. On the last day of the mission they stopped me again. Again I was with others, and they detained all of us. They marched us up to a house, and the chief, who seemed to be somebody of higher rank than the ones I'd met before, kept me for four hours, questioning me. It seems they were getting ready to attack another *campesino* co-op and were trying to prevent people from moving around. They couldn't decide whether to keep me or let me go. They kept me all night. I saw with my own eyes, and heard with my own ears, that everything they have is U.S. aid. They say it's from Reagan—'Dona Reagan.' They don't say 'Ronald Reagan,' they say 'Dona Reagan,' because their equipment is his 'donation,' his *donación*. A large shipment of things had come in that day. I'd seen the bundles drop from the plane that flew in from Honduras. They'd received cigars, matches, batteries, two-way radios. I saw the instruction sheets for the radios. They were from the United States. They apparently received a million *cordobas* that day too. They were hoping to get boots and uniforms. I saw them wearing belts that said 'United States' on them.

And it's interesting that, that night, they brought me a meal on a plate that I recognized as a special kind of thing my dad had, which can be used as a frying pan or as a plate. It's collapsible. It's U.S. army. The chief actually told me that they get everything from the United States.

"The next day they released me. They saw that I would be more trouble to keep than to let go. The people they'd abducted with me were released a few days later. But I'd like to make it public that those people are under death threat, especially the Cano Obando couple, Valentina and Nicolás, as well as the young catechist, Salvadora. I'm very much afraid for this couple and this girl. I'm afraid of their being taken again and of what might happen to them then."

"I Have a Message"

"I see and suffer these things every day. To me to call the contras 'freedom fighters,' as President Reagan does, is a cruel joke. To me, it's cruel and immoral for the United States to give the contras support and aid. It's no use trying to justify their war; they're killing and destroying the poorest of the people, the most innocent. I have a message for the United States, for those responsible for this policy, and for the people of the United States. And my message is the truth about what's happening here. But I feel so helpless. The truth doesn't get to them. They don't want to know the truth, they don't want to believe it. Just yesterday, a sister from the United States who works with me in Siuna was talking to her mom on the phone. And she can't convince her own mom! Her mom says the Sandinistas are communists, and that they're horrible, and that they should be gotten rid of. And she says it's a lie what her own daughter is telling her, who lives here in Nicaragua. The mother just blindly believes whatever the official U.S. line tells her. It's frustrating. 'But Mom,' the sister tells her, 'I live here, and I see what's happening, I see what's going on and I know the Sandinistas. They aren't the way you think they are. Things aren't the way you in the United States think they are. . . .

"We North Americans here in Nicaragua have come to the conclusion that the U.S. government is being fed a great deal of false information. For instance, everything the contra station, Radio September 15, says seems to be believed in the States. We've heard some of their reports of things that have happened in our area and they're completely false. For example, you'll hear that their forces have 'encountered large Soviet and Cuban contingents and forced them to flee in disarray.' And we *know* the people they 'encountered.' They're all Nicaraguans. Even the Nicaraguans who fought the contras have to laugh when they hear nonsense like that. They say, 'Hey, guys, did you know we're Soviets and Cubans?'

"Another true story: We have an accelerated primary program for the *campesinos* in one of our schools. One night a band of contras came and shot at us for forty minutes. Militia members returned the fire and the contras ran off. That was it. There were no casualties. Then we heard on Radio September 15 that the contras had killed eighty Sandinista soldiers and burned the school! No, the school's still there, and the forty-five *campesinos* who were there that night are all safe and sound too.

"Reports like these, false as they are, foster the Reagan policy. It's immoral. We can't let this go on.

"Aid to the contras is immoral. It's sinful. We have to learn that all the contras are doing is killing innocent people. In this war they're waging, the contras have neither the wish nor the opportunity to attack big military bases. Because they're aren't any for them to attack. We can see there aren't any! The contras swoop down on innocent people, *campesinos,* defenseless children.

"We talked to thirty-six *campesinos* who were kidnapped in August 1984, managed to escape on December 24, and wandered in the mountains, lost, till February 1. We talked to them all, from a woman who had had a baby in the mountains to tiny children who had to walk all that time. While we talked to her, the woman who gave birth in the mountains undressed her one-year-old to have something to put on the newborn baby. These are the people who have suffered. And these are the people who are expected to try to eke out a living in the face of the constant threat of incursions by the contras. This is what will continue, this and the death of the innocent, if the United States continues to give aid and assistance to the contras.

"We U.S. citizens are largely responsible for this situation of death and destruction. And we are going to be held responsible for it. Before God and in the afterlife many North Americans are going to have to pay for this."